LIBRARY OF CONGRESS

American Folklife Center

AN ILLUSTRATED GUIDE

LIBRARY OF CONGRESS   WASHINGTON   2004

*The Archive of Folk Culture
Seventy-fifth Anniversary
1928–2003*

COVER: "Echoes from the Prairie," quilt by Constance Finlayson, Carrollton, Missouri, completed June 1991. The 1992 Missouri State Winner, Lands' End All-American Quilt Contest.

Constance Finlayson made twelve blocks of antique patterns to surround a central medallion, an eight-point star, in her winning quilt design. She used "scraps and pieces" of cotton fabric from around the house, in the tradition of resourceful pioneer women. Doing all the work by hand, Finlayson described her techniques as "based on those who had gone before me—a link that bound us together." In 1997 the American Folklife Center acquired documentation from the 1992, 1994, and 1996 Lands' End All-American Quilt Contests, including images of approximately 180 winning quilts from across the United States.

This publication was made possible by generous support from the James Madison Council, a national, private-sector advisory council dedicated to helping the Library of Congress share its unique resources with the nation and the world.

The text for this guide was written by James Hardin.
Photographs of collection items were taken by David A. Taylor.
The guide was designed by Robert L. Wiser, Silver Spring, Maryland.

The text is composed in Centaur, a typeface designed by American typographer and book designer Bruce Rogers (1870–1957). The full type font was first used at the Montagne Press in 1915 for an edition of Maurice de Guérin's *The Centaur*.

LIBRARY OF CONGRESS CATALOGING-IN-PUBLICATION DATA

Library of Congress.
    Library of Congress American Folklife Center : an illustrated guide.
      p. cm.
    Written by James Hardin; photographs of collection items by David A. Taylor.
    Includes bibliographical references.
    ISBN 0-8444-1106-X (alk. paper)
    1. American Folklife Center—Handbooks, manuals, etc. 2. Folklore—United States—Handbooks, manuals, etc. 3. United States—Social life and customs—Handbooks, manuals, etc. I. Hardin, James (James B.). II. Title.
GR105.A62 2003
398'.0973—dc22

2003019727

For sale by the U.S. Government Printing Office
Superintendent of Documents
Mail Stop: SSOP, Washington, D.C. 20402–9328

Contents

FOREWORD 7
Peggy A. Bulger
Director, American Folklife Center

PREFACE 10
James Hardin
Editor, American Folklife Center

A NATIONAL PROJECT WITH MANY WORKERS 13

FOLK MUSIC AND SONG 28

STORY AND OTHER NARRATIVE FORMS 41

DANCE 51

MATERIAL CULTURE 57

COMMUNITY LIFE AND CELEBRATION 64

FOR FURTHER READING 79

MUSIC AND SPOKEN WORD FROM THE ARCHIVE OF FOLK CULTURE 80
A Compact Disc of Audio Recordings Selected by the Staff of the American Folklife Center

Foreword

THE COLLECTIONS in the American Folklife Center's Archive of Folk Culture contain one-of-a-kind documentation of traditional cultural expressions that date from the end of the nineteenth century through the dawn of the twenty-first. Today, there are more than 3 million items of ethnographic documentation in the archive, a treasure trove that represents over a hundred years of fieldwork. These collections preserve for future researchers a record of the folklife, cultural expressions, traditional arts, and oral histories of Americans and of our global neighbors. Moreover, the far-ranging work of building the Folk Archive is ongoing. The American Folklife Center is actively collecting and documenting the traditional culture of the new millennium.

The American Folklife Center, created by Congress in 1976 to "preserve and present American folklife," is proud to accept this mandate to collect, safeguard, and provide access to the unparalleled collections of the Archive of Folk Culture. The archive is an extraordinary resource for primary research on America's shared community-based heritage, innumerable personal histories, and multicultural roots. Rich and diverse, its collections provide a lasting record of American social and cultural life, a record that is truly of, by, and for the people.

Since the establishment of the Archive of American Folk-Song in 1928, the collections have grown in content and scope to include the vital documentation of traditions and culture from every corner of the nation. This list is long and includes cowboy poets, Cherokee Indian basket-makers, Cajun fiddlers, Omaha-Sioux drummers, Appalachian ballad singers, Mississippi Delta bluesmen, Adirondack storytellers, Texas barbecue masters, Italian American wine-makers, Palestinian American embroiderers, Alaskan sled-dog mushers, and Maine boatbuilders. The collections encompass and define the grassroots traditions of American life. In addition, the American Folklife Center collects materials from across the globe: documentation of traditional music and pageantry from China; everyday life, work, and celebration in Eastern Europe; music and other traditional expressions from Central America, Papua New Guinea, and Africa.

As the Library of Congress is the repository for the world's collective knowledge and achievement, so the American Folklife Center is the repository for the world's folklore, traditional wisdom, and cultural heritage. During the opening years of the twenty-first century, the archive increased its holdings by over 25 percent, and many large collections are augmented each year by additional donations. The National Council for the Traditional Arts Collection will provide an ongoing record of the outstanding folk artists in our nation. The International Storytelling Collection contains documentation of thousands of tale-tellers and folk narrators.

OPPOSITE: Bessie Collias demonstrates a join in the lace of a crocheted tablecloth at St. Nicholas Church, Chicago, Illinois, April 23, 1977. *(Chicago Ethnic Arts Project Collection. Photo by Jonas Dovydenas)*

PAGES 4–5: Robert W. Gordon, first head of the Archive of American Folk-Song at the Library of Congress, with part of the cylinder collection and recording machinery, about 1930. *(Library of Congress photo)*

The invention of the Edison cylinder recording machine in 1877 enabled folklorists and other ethnographers to make sound recordings in field settings that could be analyzed and studied carefully in another location at a later time. Robert Gordon came to the Library in 1928 to take charge of the newly created Archive of American Folk-Song, bringing with him his dream of collecting "all American folk-song."

And the Veterans History Project is the most comprehensive national oral history effort since the years of the Federal Writers Project of the 1930s—collecting the personal stories of America's living war veterans.

This illustrated guide to the American Folklife Center provides an introduction to a research collection that allows us to understand and embrace our American history and heritage, just as it offers the opportunity for us to study and better understand the many cultures of our globally linked, multicultural world. A sampling of audio recordings from the Archive of Folk Culture is provided in an accompanying compact disc.

A few thanks are in order. The creation of this American Folklife Center guide as an important addition to the Library's series of illustrated guides was encouraged and supported by former Associate Librarian of Congress Winston Tabb. James Hardin, writer and editor for the American Folklife Center, took on the job of planning, researching, writing, and coordinating the effort to make this publication a reality. Working with Director of Publishing Ralph Eubanks and editor Evelyn Sinclair of the Library of Congress Publishing Office, Jim has created a wonderful guide to a complex ethnographic collection. And finally, to all of the staff at the American Folklife Center who assisted in choosing photos, writing captions, and selecting recorded sound for the CD, a hearty thanks.

PEGGY A. BULGER
DIRECTOR
AMERICAN FOLKLIFE CENTER

OPPOSITE: Frances Densmore with Mountain Chief of the Blackfoot Tribe, who listens to a cylinder recording and translates the song into sign language, Washington, D.C., early 1900s. *(Library of Congress photo)*

Frances Densmore was a prolific collector of American Indian music who made more than twenty-five hundred wax-cylinder recordings with members of forty tribes between 1907 and the early 1940s. Her extensive collection is part of the Archive of Folk Culture.

Preface

OPPOSITE: Carrie B. Grover, Gorham, Maine, 1943. *(Eloise Hubbard Linscott Collection. Photo probably by Eloise Hubbard Linscott)*

The Eloise Hubbard Linscott Collection of New England folksongs and folklore comprises the life's work of an amateur collector devoted to the preservation of the traditional music of her region. The collection includes dictaphone cylinders, acetate discs, and audiotapes, along with field notes, transcriptions, photographic images, postcards, and other materials. A number of the discs were made with a disc-recording machine borrowed from the Library of Congress in 1941. At first, Linscott sought to gather the songs she learned as a little girl, so she could teach them to her young son. As friends and neighbors learned of her project, the collection of songs grew and eventually resulted in a book, *Folk Songs of Old New England,* published in 1939. The collection includes the performances of several New England fiddlers, including Carrie B. Grover, the only woman among them.

MOST OF THE ETHNOGRAPHIC DOCUMENTATION in the American Folklife Center's Archive of Folk Culture was created in field situations by folklorists, ethnomusicologists, anthropologists, and other cultural specialists, working either as private individuals or for the Library of Congress or other federal, state, or local agencies.

The purpose of ethnographic fieldwork is to make a systematic record of human cultural activity in its natural context, and the resulting collections may include sound recordings (in many different formats), field notes and other manuscript materials, photographs, videotapes, and ephemera. The earliest field recordings in the Archive of Folk Culture date from the 1890s; the most recent were made only a short time ago. Folklife has been defined as the "traditional, expressive culture shared within various groups," and documented in the archive is an immense variety of folklife expression, from every region of the United States, as well as from many people and cultures worldwide.

Making a survey of the visual resources of the Archive of Folk Culture was a daunting task. Folklife Center specialists were helpful in offering suggestions from the vantage points of their areas of interest and expertise. Also of great help were the many books, newsletter articles, and finding aids on particular collections, as well as a list of photographic resources in the archive prepared by Carol Moran. A number of collections are available in online versions, as part of the Library's program called American Memory: The National Digital Library. But, finally, it was necessary to open boxes and search through files to make a selection of representative and engaging images from the 3 million-item collection.

As work on the book proceeded, several members of the American Folklife Center's board of trustees suggested that a CD sampling of sound recordings might be included and, indeed, would further "illustrate" and illuminate the collections. Ralph Eubanks, director of publishing, accepted the proposal, and center staff worked together to create an audio sampling keyed as nearly as possible to references in the text of the book.

I would like to thank Peggy Bulger, director of the American Folklife Center, for her support and encouragement; and founding director Alan Jabbour for his essays on the Folk Archive and the Folklife Center, which served as the basis for the history chapter in this guide.

For their help in making suggestions, reading text, and preparing captions, I would like to thank the following: Peggy Bulger, Jennifer Cutting, Judith Gray, Stephanie Hall, Todd Harvey, Joseph C. Hickerson, Michael Taft, David A. Taylor, and Nora Yeh. In addition, David Taylor suggested folklife expressions as

the organizing principle for the guide and was an especially discerning final reader. Todd Harvey took on a number of assignments, particularly in the area of caption writing. Contributing to the production of the CD were Jennifer Cutting, Judith Gray, Todd Harvey, Ann Hoog, Michael Taft, and Jonathan Gold, who served as audio technician. Evelyn Sinclair, Publishing Office editor, colleague, and friend, guided this project from the start.

JAMES HARDIN
EDITOR, AMERICAN FOLKLIFE CENTER

A National Project with Many Workers

In 1928, when the Librarian of Congress, Herbert Putnam, invited Robert W. Gordon to become "specialist and consultant in the field of Folk Song and Literature," Gordon had already conceived and launched his lifetime mission to collect the entire body of American folk music. He called it a "national project with many workers." Gordon attended Harvard University between 1906 and 1917 as an undergraduate and graduate student in English, and then left in order to devote all his free time to this collecting enterprise. Supporting himself through teaching, writing, and the occasional grant, Gordon traveled from the waterfronts of Oakland and San Francisco, California, to Asheville, North Carolina, and Darien, Georgia, collecting and recording folksongs with his Edison wax-cylinder machine. He wrote a monthly column in *Adventure* magazine, "Old Songs That Men Have Sung," asking readers to send in copies of all the folksongs they could remember. And he contacted Carl Engel, chief of the Music Division at the Library of Congress, to discuss his dream and seek institutional support.

Engel believed that American grassroots traditions should be represented in the national library, and wrote in *The Annual Report of the Librarian of Congress* for 1928:

There is a pressing need for the formation of a great centralized collection of American folk-songs. The logical place for such a collection is the national library of the United States. This collection should comprise all the poems and melodies that have sprung from our soil or have been transplanted here, and have been handed down, often with manifold changes, from generation to generation as a precious possession of our folk.

Countless individuals, numerous walks of life, several races have contributed to this treasure of songs and ballads. It is richer than that of any other country. Too much of it has remained scattered or unrecorded. The preservation of this material in the remote haunts where it still flourishes is endangered by the spread of the radio and phonograph, which are diverting the attention of the people from their old heritage and are making them less dependent on it.

The Library of Congress is vitally interested in the collecting of these folk verses and folk melodies. The collecting must be done in a scholarly manner and the collection, safeguarded against improper use, should be made freely accessible to scholars.

Robert Gordon was not the first to use the latest technology to document our national traditional culture, nor Carl Engel the first to acknowledge its importance. Thomas A. Edison invented the cylinder recording machine in 1877, and it became available commercially about 1888. The machine facilitated documentary work by many private individuals, as well as those employed by government agencies and public museums. These ethnographers shared a common vision. They believed that the history of the American nation ought to include the

OPPOSITE: John A. Lomax *(left)* and Uncle Rich Brown at the home of Mrs. Julia Killingsworth, near Sumterville, Alabama, October 1940. *(Prints and Photographs Division)*

John A. Lomax was head of the Archive of American Folk-Song (1932–42) but spent most of his time away from Washington, often in the field. Sumter County, Alabama, which lies along the southwest border of the state, proved to be one of Lomax's most fertile collecting locations. During his trip there, October–November 1940, accompanied by his wife Ruby Terrill Lomax and Mrs. Ruby Pickens Tartt of the Alabama Federal Writer's Project, Lomax recorded Rich Brown singing eleven songs, many of them spirituals.

Alan Lomax with guitar, in a publicity photo, 1940. *(American Folklife Center)*

Alan Lomax is best known as a folksong collector, but during his tenure at the Library of Congress he also worked the lecture circuit, gave concerts, and made recordings. This is a publicity photo for his work with the Columbia Lecture Bureau in 1940. His association with the bureau probably derived from his radio series *Columbia's School of the Air.* The Lecture Bureau said of Alan Lomax, "With his records and his guitar he brings his listeners closer to America, the real America . . . close to the singing country that he believes America to be."

many voices of its diverse population, a notion that later figured in the creation of the American Folklife Center. They believed that sound—both song and spoken word—was a vital part of the historical, cultural record.

Harvard anthropologist Jesse Walter Fewkes was the first to use the Edison cylinder machine for ethnographic research. Field recordings made on wax cylinders could be brought back to a studio for study, and Fewkes used Edison's machine in Maine, in 1890, to record the songs and stories of Passamaquoddy Indians. These wax cylinder recordings, the first ethnographic recordings extant, are in the collections of the Archive of Folk Culture. Between 1907 and the early 1940s, Frances Densmore collected more than twenty-five hundred recordings from members of forty tribes. She was one of a number of pioneering women in the field of ethnographic documentation (including Alice Cunningham Fletcher, Helen Heffron Roberts, and Laura Bolton) whose collections are now in the Archive of Folk Culture.

THE ARCHIVE OF FOLK CULTURE

When the Archive of American Folk-Song was first established in the Music Division, it was funded from private sources. Periodic disagreements over his methods erupted between Robert Gordon and Library of Congress officials during his tenure as head, and the private money that Carl Engel had secured to fund Gordon's position eventually came to an end. But the idea of a national folk archive had taken root, and it was revived when John A. Lomax came to the Library in 1932. Lomax too was devoted to collecting American folksong, and the decade-long association of John A. Lomax and his son, Alan, with the Library of Congress established the documentation of traditional culture as an important and integral activity of the institution.

Alan Lomax became the Folk Archive's first federally funded staff member in 1936, and, beginning in 1937, served as "assistant in charge." He made collecting expeditions for the Library throughout the South, in the Midwest, and in New England; produced a seminal series of documentary folk music albums entitled *Folk Music of the United States*; conducted interviews with performers, such as Jelly Roll Morton; and, over the years, introduced audiences in Washington, D.C., and radio listeners nationwide to an array of traditional artists.

An arrangement with the Library initiated by John A. Lomax, wherein he would "give to the Library, in return for the use of a recording machine, any records that he might obtain with it" (*Report of the Librarian of Congress for the Fiscal*

Year Ending June 30, 1933), facilitated his own collecting activities and launched a documentary equipment-loan program that has lasted for seventy years. Using successive types of equipment from the Library, as recording technologies evolved from cylinder to disc to tape, collectors such as Vance Randolph, Charles Todd, Robert Sonkin, Eloise Hubbard Linscott, Zora Neale Hurston, Herbert Halpert, William Fenton, Melville Herskovits, Helen Hartness Flanders, Austin Fife, and many others were able to pursue their personal collecting activities and, at the same time, contribute to the national collection. The strategy of lending equipment and recording supplies to a network of regional collectors was enormously productive, both in building the collection and in creating a community of folklorists with ties to the Library.

The desire to distribute the Folk Archive's holdings for public and educational uses led to the creation of the Library's Recording Laboratory, which produced the first releases in the Folk Music of the United States series in 1942. In the 1950s, the early 78-rpm albums were converted to 33-rpm, and new LP releases appeared through the early 1980s. As new technologies developed for making field recordings—wax cylinder, disc, wire, tape, and so forth—the laboratory staff acquired machines, developed expertise, and initiated publishing projects to make available to the public traditional music that was thought at the

Folklorist Herbert Halpert poses by the old ambulance he outfitted as a "sound wagon," using an acetate-disc recorder borrowed from the Archive of American Folk-Song. Saltillo, Mississippi, 1939. *(Photo courtesy of Mississippi Department of Archives and History)*

Herbert Halpert was one of the many folklorists of his generation to profit from the Library of Congress's Equipment Loan Program. Halpert's work was also supported through contracts with the Library and other federal agencies, including the Works Progress Administration (WPA) during the Great Depression. He traveled throughout the southern United States, amassing more than four hundred discs of songs and music.

HEADS OF THE ARCHIVE OF FOLK CULTURE

Robert W. Gordon (1928–32)

John A. Lomax (1933–42, keeping the title "honorary curator" until his death in 1948)

Alan Lomax (1937–42, with the title "assistant in charge")

Benjamin A. Botkin (1942–45)

Duncan Emrich (1945–55, with the title "chief of the Folklore Section")

Rae Korson (1956–69)

Alan Jabbour (1969–74)

Joseph C. Hickerson (1974–88)

Alan Jabbour (1988–99, as director of the American Folklife Center)

Peggy Bulger (1999–2002, as director of the American Folklife Center)

Michael Taft (2002–   )

time to have no commercial value. It was also necessary for the laboratory to buy and maintain recording equipment associated with each succeeding technology. In the 1990s, CD versions of many of these early recordings, as well as new releases from the world music collections, were produced and distributed through cooperative agreements with commercial recording companies.

The expertise developed by the Recording Laboratory, the equipment-loan program, and the growing reputation of the Library of Congress as a repository for ethnographic documentation were appealing to folklorists and cultural documentarians working in this country and in foreign lands as well. Library of Congress collections are international in scope, and Library officials supported an international acquisition policy for the Folk Archive. A recording trip to the Bahamas that Alan Lomax made in 1935, during his tenure at the Library, may have been the first instance of seeking folklife materials from outside the United States. The Folk Archive now holds material from nearly every region in the world.

During the 1940s and 1950s, for example, Arthur S. Alberts made remarkable recordings of West African music, from a dozen ethnic groups and six different colonial territories, all of which he contributed to the Library of Congress during the tenure of archive head Duncan Emrich. When portions of this collection were made available commercially, they did much to counter stereotypical notions about the "Dark Continent" by presenting examples of authentic cultural expressions. During her long career, anthropologist Henrietta Yurchenco has documented the traditions of African Americans on John's Island, South Carolina, and in Puerto Rico. She has also conducted fieldwork in Mexico, Guatemala, Spain, Morocco, and Ireland. Like many such collectors of international folklife materials, Yurchenco has made periodic donations to the Library of Congress.

The Folk Archive also received an infusion of material when John A. Lomax, Benjamin A. Botkin (who followed Alan Lomax as head of the archive), and others associated with the Folk Archive participated in New Deal-era programs such as the Federal Writers' Project. During the 1930s, hundreds of federal workers were employed in cultural projects around the country, including the Ex-Slave Narrative Project and the California Folk Music Project. When the Work Projects Administration (WPA) offices finally closed down, in response to a shifting of emphasis to national defense as the United States entered the Second World War, Library of Congress officials facilitated the transfer of cultural materials collected by its various agencies to the Library.

Thus, by the 1940s, the Archive of American Folk-Song had expanded its documentary scope to include folklore, verbal arts, and oral history. In addition

Henrietta Yurchenco *(right)* and an unidentified woman, near Zion Methodist Church, John's Island, South Carolina, March 1970. *(Henrietta Yurchenco Collection. Photo by David Lewiston)*

Henrietta Yurchenco began doing fieldwork in 1942 in Mexico and Guatemala, where she recorded traditional music in Indian communities. On a 1970 visit to John's Island, South Carolina, Professor Yurchenco brought some of her undergraduate students from the City College of New York to help her record music during spring recess. There, the students experienced first-hand the civil rights movement as it was taking place at a church that was spearheading a drive to register black voters. The Reverend Goodwin preached an impassioned Easter Sunday sermon on civil rights at Zion Methodist Church that weekend.

Helen Hartness Flanders with three New England folksingers in the Coolidge Auditorium of the Library of Congress, 1948. *(Library of Congress photo)*

In 1948, Vermont folksong collector Helen Hartness Flanders, wife of Vermont senator Ralph Flanders, presented a lecture and concert of New England ballads, sung by three folksingers, in the Coolidge Auditorium. The singers are *(front row, left to right)* Charles Fennimore (from Maine), Elmer George, and Asa Davis (both from Vermont). Behind them, standing, are Charles Spivacke, chief of the Music Division; Helen Hartness Flanders; and Duncan Emrich, chief of the Folklore Section. Alan Lomax, with whom Flanders consulted regarding her own collecting efforts in Vermont, staged the first folk music program at the Library in 1940.

to his work as "assistant in charge" at the archive, Alan Lomax was hosting and producing programs for the *CBS School of the Air* in New York City, and participating in the Rockefeller Foundation-funded Radio Research Project at the Library of Congress. One activity of the project was to conduct recorded interviews that sampled public opinion from around the country, and the day after the attack on Pearl Harbor, December 7, 1941, Lomax put out a call for folklorists to collect "man on the street" reactions to the event. Sixty years later, the American Folklife Center followed Lomax's example by asking folklorists from across the nation to document immediate public reactions to the tragic events of September 11, 2001.

With national energies focused on the Second World War, folklife collecting activities slowed, but successive Folk Archive heads continued the policies and practices established by the Lomaxes—lending documentation equipment and supplies, publishing materials from the collections, and encouraging donations of material from this country and around the world. Benjamin A. Botkin helped to redefine and broaden the purview of folklore research to include ethnic studies and cultural traditions found in urban settings. He also encouraged folklorists to become involved in public performances and presentations by traditional artists. He is best known for his many popular anthologies, such as the *Treasury of American Folklore* (1944) and *Lay My Burden Down* (1945), which draws on the Folk Archive's recordings of ex-slave narratives.

Duncan Emrich was another Harvard-trained folklorist and historian (like Robert Gordon, John Lomax, and Benjamin Botkin) who advanced Folk Archive acquisition efforts. The growing reputation of the archive following World War II resulted in a flood of requests for reference information and services, both from private individuals and from radio, motion picture, and publishing firms. Emrich argued vigorously for a larger staff to help respond to the many demands of acquisition, processing, and reference. The Library failed to hire additional staff but did name Emrich chief of a Folklore Section created within the Music Division. (The unit was abandoned after Emrich's departure.) Emrich developed a visionary four-year plan for acquiring recordings from twelve states whose traditional culture was not represented in the archive, with particular emphasis on narrative, occupational culture, and materials from urban areas and minority language groups. He also proposed documenting traditional performers from foreign lands, such as Asia, Africa, the Pacific, and Australia. To facilitate his plan, Emrich visited twenty-one colleges and universities around the country to initiate a network of university-based documentary programs and to urge the creation of state folklore archives.

A new generation of regional collectors was at work following World War II. Wayland Hand was working among the miners in Butte, Montana; Arthur Campa, collecting Hispanic songs in New Mexico; and Thelma James, recording among the minority communities in Detroit. The Archive of Folk Culture profited from all this effort, and collections eventually arrived at the Library, on the new documentary medium of tape, from Anne Grimes (Ohio folksongs), Ray B. Browne (Alabama folklife), Sherman Lee Pompey (folksongs and folklore from the Ozarks), Joseph S. Hall (folklife from the Smokey Mountains of Tennessee), Harry Oster (Iowa and Louisiana cultural traditions), and Alan Jabbour (fiddling traditions, featuring the legendary Henry Reed of Glen Lyn, Virginia).

In the Library's annual report for 1950, halfway through his tenure as head, Duncan Emrich reported that the number of discs in the collection had reached ten thousand, and that henceforth the medium of choice for the documentation of sound would be tape recordings. Significantly, he reported to the Librarian, Luther Evans:

It is possible to say, in 1950, that the pioneering phase of field collecting and the establishment of Archives has come to a close and that in the future emphasis should be directed to coordinated efforts, to elimination of duplication, and to strong encouragement for scholars and others to use—in fairly exhaustive studies—the materials already gathered.

In 1955, when Emrich resigned his position, his assistant, Rae Korson, was named head of the Folk Archive. Her husband, folklorist George Korson, documented songs and lore of Pennsylvania coal miners, and that work is included in the archive today. Rae Korson, who held a degree in law, had served as assistant and reference librarian to both Botkin and Emrich. In her new position, she stressed the importance of maintenance and preservation of the vast holdings that had accumulated, an emphasis that was consistent with the policies of L. Quincy Mumford, then Librarian of Congress. She was particularly interested in improving reference service and publishing additional recordings from the Folk Archive. In 1963, Korson hired Joseph C. Hickerson (to take the place of reference librarian Donald Leavitt) and Pat Markland (to fill a new position as secretary), bringing the staff to three. Hickerson himself would later become head of what was by then called the Archive of Folk Song.

Alan Jabbour followed Korson as head (1969–74). He had both strong academic credentials and fieldwork experience, and in keeping with his own interests as a folksong collector he resumed the practice of making field expeditions. With Carl Fleischhauer, he conducted a field project in West Virginia, from 1970 to 1972, to study the expressive traditions of the Hammons family of Pocahontas County, and this effort resulted in a boxed-set of two-LP recordings (1973) consisting of music, song, storytelling, and oral history. In addition, Jabbour traveled to various places in pursuit of important collections, and he acquired significant holdings in Native American traditional culture, including a small collection of early cylinders from the Peabody Museum of Harvard University, among them Jesse Walter Fewkes's 1890 recordings of Passamaquoddy Indians. In 1972, Jabbour also acquired a large and important collection documenting songs, ballads, and folk plays of the British Isles from the American folklorist James Madison Carpenter, an effort inspired by a letter he discovered in the Folk Archive from Carpenter to Alan Lomax. The elderly Carpenter had disappeared from the scene twenty years earlier, but through the Harvard University Alumni Association Jabbour was able to track him to his home in Booneville, Mississippi, and purchase the collection for the archive.

The 1950s and 1960s spawned a folksong revival in the United States that included the release of commercial recordings from many popular performers and

Bluesman Mississippi John Hurt, Rae Korson *(left)*, and Joseph C. Hickerson *(center)*, in the Library of Congress Recording Laboratory, March 17, 1964. *(Library of Congress photo)*

Mississippi John Hurt made a number of commercial recordings in 1928, but farmed for a living, never pursuing music professionally. In the early 1960s, a fan of Hurt's music contacted and convinced him to travel to Washington and record for the Library of Congress.

groups, a proliferation of coffeehouse "folksingers," and spontaneous hootenannies everywhere. The Folk Archive both nourished and profited from this renewed interest and the new popularity of music with traditional roots. The collections were a resource for performers of many sorts seeking examples of traditional musical performance, and the Folk Archive gained attention that brought in new collections.

In 1974 Alan Jabbour moved to the National Endowment for the Arts to direct its newly created Folk Arts Program, and Joseph C. Hickerson became head of the Folk Archive. Hickerson did much to argue the case for the importance of documenting and collecting material from the folksong revival. Folk festivals were enormously popular during the 1970s, and Hickerson encouraged donations of material documenting the movement. Under Hickerson's leadership, special emphasis was placed on the organization and cataloging of the archive's collections, the creation of listening tapes to facilitate the study of the holdings by visiting scholars, and the further production and dissemination of recordings. Between 1974 and 1976, as part of its American Revolution Bicentennial program, the Library of Congress issued the first five albums in a new fifteen-album series Folk Music of America, with a grant from the National Endowment for the Arts.

The American Folklife Center

During the decade preceding the establishment of the American Folklife Center in 1976, a number of factors conjoined to bring about the legislation that created it. In 1967 the Smithsonian Festival of American Folklife was held for the first time on the National Mall, bringing a wide range of traditional artists to Washington and winning enthusiastic congressional support. About the same time, the approaching American Revolution Bicentennial stimulated a reexamination of pluralism in American life. A number of dedicated people, notably folklorist and labor historian Archie Green, walked the halls of Congress to lobby for congressional recognition of the importance of regional and ethnic cultures. Many cultural specialists believed the time was right for a national center devoted to the preservation and study of folklife.

The American Folklife Preservation Act, Public Law 94–201, which resulted from these efforts, defines the term "American folklife" as "the traditional expressive culture shared within the various groups in the United States: familial, ethnic, occupational, religious, regional." It states that "the diversity inherent in American folklife has contributed greatly to the cultural richness of the Nation and has fostered a sense of individuality and identity among the American people."

The American Folklife Preservation Act was approved by both houses of Congress at the end of 1975, and signed into law by President Gerald Ford on January 2, 1976. The legislation created an American Folklife Center and charged the new organization to "preserve and present American folklife." Initially intended for the Smithsonian Institution, the center was placed in the Library of Congress, in part to build upon the work of the Folk Archive already there.

The Folklife Center operates under the supervision of the Librarian of Congress and a board of trustees composed of individuals from private life appointed by the Speaker of the U.S. House of Representatives, the president pro tempore of the Senate, and the Librarian of Congress; officials from federal agencies with cultural programs, appointed by the president of the United States; and ex officio members—the Librarian of Congress, the secretary of the Smithsonian Institution, the chairs of the National Endowment for the Arts and the National Endowment for the Humanities, the director of the American Folklife Center, and the presidents of the Society for Ethnomusicology and the American Folklore Society.

The Folklife Center's enabling legislation directs it to "preserve and present American folklife" through programs of research, scholarship, training, live

Folklorist Beverly Robinson (right) with Jessie Lee Smith, on the porch of his home, Tifton, Georgia, August 1977. (South-Central Georgia Folklife Project Collection. Photo by Carl Fleischhauer)

For its cultural surveys and field projects, the American Folklife Center formed teams of field-workers, led by one or more members of its own staff but also including cultural specialists from the local area and from other parts of the country. The South-Central Georgia project was initiated by the Arts Experiment Station at Abraham Baldwin Agricultural College and conducted in cooperation with local arts and governmental agencies.

The Bluegrass Cardinals, from Virginia, on the steps of the Thomas Jefferson Building, April 25, 1977. *(Library of Congress photo)*

The popularity of a concert on the Neptune Plaza, in front of the Library's Thomas Jefferson Building, presented on September 23, 1976, led to the creation of an annual series, inaugurated the following year. Over the years, the Neptune Plaza Concert Series has entertained and enlightened audiences with a diverse assortment of traditional music and dance from this country and around the world.

performances, exhibits, publications, and preservation. The legislation also calls for the establishment and maintenance of a national archive "with any Federal department, agency, or institution." But, of course, a folk archive was near at hand, and the Archive of Folk Culture was transferred from the Music Division to the center in 1978. Thus, the traditional archival activities of acquisition, processing, preservation, and reference have remained central to the mission and the daily life of the American Folklife Center.

In September 1976, Alan Jabbour, who had served earlier as head of the Folk Archive, became the first director of the American Folklife Center. In 1977, the first full year of its operations, the center launched two field documentary projects, the Chicago Ethnic Arts Project and the South-Central Georgia Folklife Project, setting a pattern that came to characterize much of its early work. One project was urban and one rural, but both emphasized the importance of documenting artistic traditions professionally, using both sound recordings and still photography, with an eye both to creating public products such as books and exhibitions and to building the collections in the Folk Archive. Teams of center field-workers sought to document not only music but also verbal arts, material culture, and occupational traditions, as well as other aspects of culture.

The creation of the American Folklife Center also engaged the U.S. Congress in the folklore enterprise. Whereas most Folk Archive collections had resulted from the vision and interest of individuals—both private citizens and those working for government agencies and large public institutions—many of the center's field documentary projects were now carried out in cooperation with the National Park Service, often at the behest of a member (or members) of Congress. The center has worked with the Park Service on cultural heritage surveys in northern Maine; Lowell, Massachusetts; the New Jersey Pine Barrens and Paterson, New Jersey; along the Blue Ridge Parkway, in Virginia and North Carolina; and at New River Gorge, in West Virginia.

In 1979, the Folklife Center launched the Federal Cylinder Project, one of its most ambitious undertakings. Over the decades, the Folk Archive had received thousands of original, one-of-a-kind wax-cylinder recordings of ethnographic material from field documentation conducted from 1890 through the 1930s, primarily of American Indian music. The Library's Recording Laboratory had developed a special expertise in the technically challenging work of copying these recordings. In the 1930s and 1940s, some were copied onto disc, and beginning in the 1960s others were copied onto magnetic tape. Now a commitment was made to copy all of the more than ten thousand wax cylinders and cylinder-based recordings in the archive for preservation and access. Word of the project brought even more cylinders to the Library.

The Federal Cylinder Project was established to arrange, catalog, and transfer to preservation tape this priceless heritage of music. In addition, the project made cassette-tape copies of the recordings to return to the tribes of origin. This last activity exemplified a central philosophical tenet of the Folk Archive and of many ethnographic archives throughout the United State, that the documentary materials ultimately belong to the communities of origin. For many years, representatives of American Indian tribes have visited the American Folklife Center to use the collections for their own programs of cultural preservation and revitalization.

Since the Folklife Center's establishment in 1976, the Folk Archive has grown dramatically, both from the field documentation initiatives undertaken by the center itself and from the acquisition of major collections. By 1981, the archive was officially named the Archive of Folk Culture to reflect the breadth of its collections. In July 1999 Peggy A. Bulger succeeded Alan Jabbour as director of the American Folklife Center. In October 1999, the center was granted permanent authorization by the U.S. Congress. In 2002, Michael Taft was appointed head of the Folk Archive.

Today, the archive contains more than 3 million items and is truly the national folk archive of the United States. In keeping with the multicultural character of American society and the international scope of the Library of Congress, its holdings also encompass folklife materials from around the world. Yet many items in this storehouse of information are imperiled because of the fragile nature of sound recordings. In urgent need of preservation are thousands of original audio recordings made over the course of the twentieth century by folklorists, ethnomusicologists, anthropologists, and other ethnographers, on wax cylinder, wire, aluminum disc, acetate, audiotape, and videotape. Many, including those from the past several decades, require immediate conservation treatment and copying to other formats. Also in need of preservation are scores of photographs, drawings, diagrams, maps, and field notes that complement and provide interpretive information on the recordings.

In July 2000, a project proposed jointly by the American Folklife Center in the Library of Congress and the Center for Folklife and Cultural Heritage of the Smithsonian Institution was awarded a grant of $750,000 to preserve the historic sound recordings housed at the two institutions. The White House Millennium Council's preservation program Save America's Treasures, in partnership with the National Park Service and the National Trust for Historic Preservation, made the grant.

Among its several aims, the Save Our Sounds audio preservation project, as it came to be called, serves as a model and is building expertise at the American Folklife Center that can then be shared with others. All ethnographic collections will have to face the inevitable deterioration of their sound recordings, and all will need standards and guidelines for preservation. If the last hundred years have been a time of great accumulation of recorded sound, then the twenty-first century promises to be a time of major preservation of sound recordings to ensure that they remain accessible.

The American Folklife Center is a small agency with a very large mission. The Library of Congress provides essential institutional support, of course, but to extend its reach the center engages in cooperative agreements with other public and private organizations, such as those with the National Park Service for field documentation projects and others with commercial firms for various print and music recording publication projects. For example, the center has a cooperative arrangement with the International Storytelling Foundation of Jonesborough, Tennessee, to collect, preserve, and disseminate information about storytelling. The center has likewise acquired thousands of hours of audio and video recordings, photographs, manuscripts, and publications from

Federal Cylinder Project sound technician and folklorist Erika Brady, in the Recording Laboratory of the Library of Congress (circa 1980), makes a copy of a wax-cylinder recording using a reel-to-reel tape machine. *(American Folklife Center photo by Carl Fleischhauer)*

The American Folklife Center is one of the world's foremost repositories of early wax-cylinder field recordings documenting the music and lore of Native American cultures, among them many recordings transferred from the Smithsonian Institution's Bureau of American Ethnology. By the early 1970s it was clear that time was taking its toll on the cylinders and preservation duplication was urgent. Renewed interest on the part of American Indian tribes in their own cultural heritage heightened the need to preserve and catalog this extensive collection.

the National Storytelling Festival. Through an innovative arrangement with the National Council for the Traditional Arts, based in Silver Spring, Maryland, the center is acquiring a vast collection of five thousand hours of recordings from the National Folk Festival and other events.

In November 2000, the American Folklife Center launched the Veterans History Project, which was authorized by Public Law 106–380. Approved by President Bill Clinton on October 27, 2000, the Veterans History Project is designed to collect and preserve the personal stories of America's war veterans and to make selections from these stories available on the Internet. This immense project has been undertaken with the cooperation and participation of many project partners, including the military service organizations and numerous individual volunteers, and is supported by a major grant from AARP.

Thus does the American Folklife Center find itself newly engaged in its mission "to preserve and present American folklife" in the new millennium, as it continues to fulfill the dream of the Folk Archive's first inspired collector, Robert W. Gordon, who sought to gather together in a national archive all our songs and stories, a great task he regarded as "a national project with many workers."

Peter Alyea, digital conversion specialist and sound engineer in the Library's Motion Picture, Broadcasting, and Recorded Sound Division, transfers the sound from a disc recording to a digital file. *(American Folklife Center photo by James Hardin, February 2003)*

The American Folklife Center's Save Our Sounds Project is preserving as digital files many thousands of endangered audio recordings, made in different formats, from the 1890s to the present.

Folk Music and Song

OPPOSITE: Frank Proffitt sings and plays for Anne Warner in 1941. Pick Britches Valley, North Carolina. *(Frank Warner Collection. Photo by Frank Warner)*

Frank Proffitt, of isolated Pick Britches Valley in western North Carolina, married into the Hicks family, well-known in the area for their musicianship and storytelling. Anne and Frank Warner had become enamored of a dulcimer made by Nathan Hicks, and in 1938 they traveled from their home in New York to Beech Mountain, North Carolina, for the first of several collecting trips. Frank Proffitt played a number of songs for them, including "Tom Dula," a nineteenth-century local murder ballad. Twenty years later, the Kingston Trio's recording "Tom Dooley" shot to the top of the popular charts, bringing traditional music and the name of Frank Proffitt to a new, mainstream audience, and contributing significantly to the 1960s folk revival.

BEGINNING IN 1929, when she collected her first folksong from fellow Vermonter Dorothy Canfield Fisher, Helen Hartness Flanders devoted thirty years of her life to finding and recording thousands of folksongs and ballads as performed by traditional singers from Vermont and other New England states. She said that she was "allergic" to ballads: whenever she got near them she caught them. The history of the Archive of Folk Culture begins as a story of "song-catchers."

A year earlier, in 1928, when Robert W. Gordon came to the Library of Congress as head of the newly created Archive of American Folk-Song, he brought with him his dream of collecting all American folksongs. While other collectors were typically interested in finding surviving examples of English and Scottish ballads, and were primarily interested in the academic study of song texts, Gordon collected a wide range of songs from a variety of informants. Furthermore, Gordon made sound recordings of the traditional singers he found, in order to secure not just song texts but also their melodies.

Texas folklorist John A. Lomax feared that the radio and gramophone would discourage people from making their own music, and that songs would be forgotten and lost. During the 1930s and 1940s he carried a recording machine throughout the South, traveling with his son Alan (as well as with his first wife, Bess, and later his second wife, Ruby). The Lomaxes visited farms and ranches, schoolyards and churches, night clubs and prisons. Working together and separately, father and son recorded cowboy ballads, work songs, religious songs, field hollers, blues, and many other forms of traditional expression. They were tireless collectors with an uncanny knack for finding traditional singers with large repertoires, and convincing them to sing and play for the cumbersome disc-cutting machine they carried with them.

Ballad scholarship in the United States traces its origin to Francis James Child, of Harvard's Department of English. Child was the editor of *The English and Scottish Popular Ballads* (1882–84). Folklore studies are frequently associated with departments of English, and both Robert Gordon and John Lomax were encouraged to pursue their interest in folksong by Harvard English professors George Lyman Kittredge and Barrett Wendell. But most American song-catchers, who exploited successive recording technologies beginning with Edison's wax-cylinder machine, were more than literary scholars. They believed their work had a moral importance that transcended academic study.

Operating from motives similar to those of other ethnographers, Frances Densmore, Helen Heffron Roberts, Willard Rhodes, and others documented

LEFT: *Walking for Dat Cake Songster,* "Containing a full collection of new songs, jokes, stump speeches, which have made Harrigan & Hart the champions of the day, among which will be found the following songs...." Compiled by Edward Harrigan and Tony Hart (New York: A.J. Fisher, 1877). *(Robert W. Gordon Songster Collection)*

RIGHT: *Gliding Down the Stream Songster,* which "Contains an unusually large collection of the best of the latest songs, jokes, and stump speeches...," compiled by Edward Harrigan and Tony Hart (New York: A.J. Fisher, 1877). *(Robert W. Gordon Songster Collection)*

American songsters are pocket-sized collections of texts of vaudeville, minstrel-stage, patriotic, religious, and sometimes traditional songs, presented without music. Popular in the United States in the nineteenth century, songsters were cheaply printed and distributed in large quantities. They were used for promotional purposes by the manufacturers of medicines, tonics, or elixirs; by distributors of other consumable goods; or by popular stage entertainers. Sometimes they were produced by music publishers who used them as samplers of their products. Archive head Robert W. Gordon himself amassed many of the songsters in the extensive collection of about seven hundred songsters, and some may have been sent to him in response to the advertisements he took out asking people for copies of folksongs.

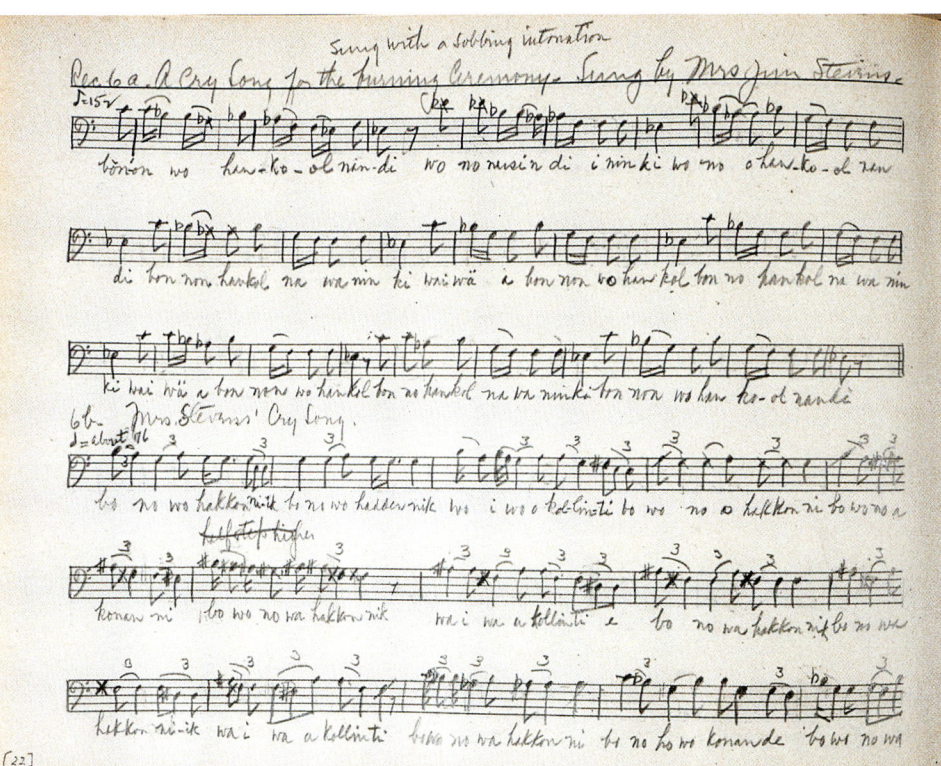

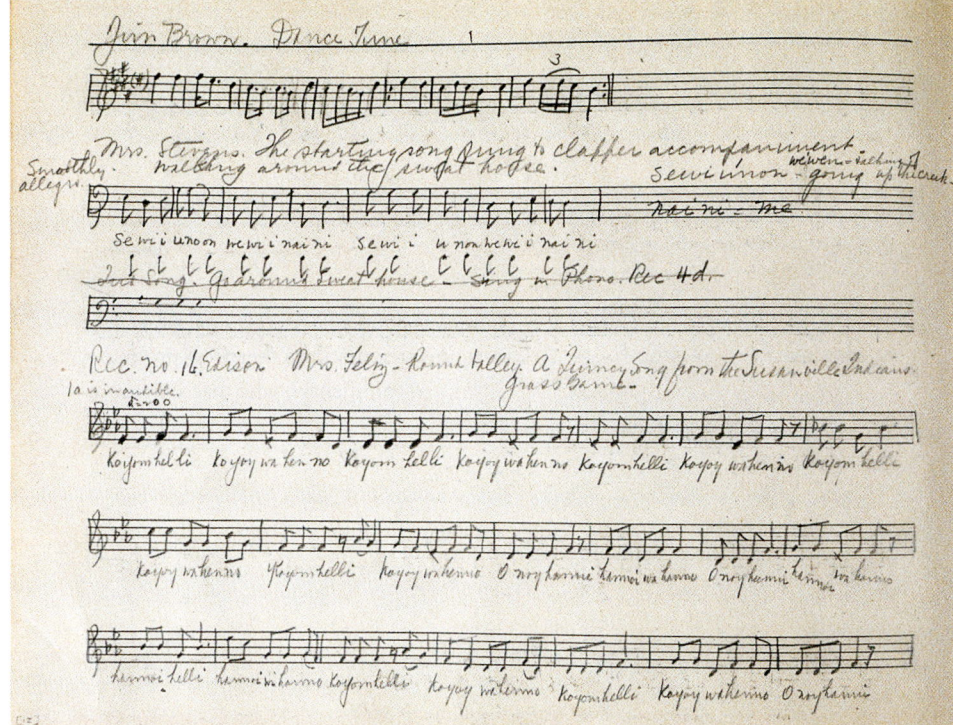

Handwritten pages from Helen Heffron Roberts's Round Valley, California, notebooks, 1926, containing transcriptions of two Konkow Burning Ceremony cry songs from wax cylinder recordings made by Mrs. Jim Stevens and of a Grass Game song from the Maidu area recorded by Anna Feliz. *(Helen Heffron Roberts Collection)*

Helen Heffron Roberts was a pioneer ethnomusicologist, known primarily for her work in native Californian communities in the 1920s and 1930s, some of it done in collaboration with John Peabody Harrington. Trained in music as well as in anthropology, Roberts made detailed transcriptions of the field recordings of native music collected by others—including James Murie's Pawnee recordings, Edward Sapir's Nootka recordings, and the Copper Eskimo recordings gathered by Diamond Jenness. Her own field recordings are usually accompanied by field notes and musical transcriptions.

Wes Noel plays the fiddle, Elk Springs, Missouri. *(Vance Randolph Collection. Photo by Vance Randolph)*

Among the most important regional folklorists working in North America during the twentieth century, Vance Randolph became known as "Mr. Ozark." He wrote on a wide range of topics, including philosophy, religion, firearms, and western outlaws. He wrote biographies, novels, short stories, and poetry, and met or corresponded with literary luminaries of his day such as H. L. Mencken, Carl Sandburg, and Theodore Dreiser. In 1941, Randolph contracted with the Library of Congress to collect folksongs using a disc-cutting machine supplied to him by Alan Lomax through the Folk Archive's Equipment Loan Program. Randolph sent back more than eight hundred songs and fiddle tunes. In addition, the Vance Randolph Collection comprises photographs of performers such as Wes Noel, extensive correspondence, and newspaper clippings and other printed materials.

Native American music, fearing that American Indians displaced from their lands were also in danger of losing their culture. The sound recording was especially important for this work, since Indian song texts are frequently composed not of words found in the singer's spoken language but of vocables, nonlexical syllables, such as *hey* or *na*, that fall into patterns shaped by linguistic, song genre, and musical considerations.

Traditional singers (or musicians or storytellers) are those who have learned their art informally, within the context of family, tribe, community, or another close-knit group. Many traditional songs have been sung within the same family or folk group for generations, and can sometimes be traced back to such places of origin as Great Britain, Europe, or Africa. At some point the song would have been composed by a single individual, but that author may no longer be known. Most folksongs change over time, to a lesser or greater extent, as they are passed from person to person and multiple variants spring up.

In some contexts, traditional songs are an integral part of daily life, and particular songs are performed to accompany particular activities associated with work, religious celebration, or social occasions. Anglo-American ballads often offer cautionary tales and moral lessons, warning young women about the temptations of honey-tongued suitors and warning men about the wiles of unfaithful

Myrtle B. Wilkinson plays tenor banjo, Turlock, California, 1939. *(WPA California Folk Music Project Collection. Photographer unknown)*

From 1938 to 1940, folksong collector Sidney Robertson organized and directed a California Work Projects Administration project designed to survey musical traditions in northern California. Sponsored by the Music Department of the University of California, Berkeley, and cosponsored by the Library of Congress, the New York Music Society, and the Society of California Pioneers, the project was one of the earliest attempts to conduct a large-scale survey of American folk music in a defined region. About a third of the thirty-five hours of instantaneous sound recordings Sidney Robertson made on 12-inch acetate discs are English-language material. The other two-thirds are the vocal and instrumental performances of numerous ethnic groups (primarily European), including Armenians, Basques, Croatians, Finns, Hungarians, Icelanders, Italians, Norwegians, Russian Molokans, and Scots. Portuguese music from the Azores and Spanish music from Mexico, Puerto Rico, and Spain are included. In addition to the recordings, the WPA California Folk Music Project Collection contains Sidney Robertson's excellent field notes, which record her ethnographic and personal impressions, many fine photographs of the performers, and drawings of instruments.

RIGHT: Huddie "Leadbelly" Ledbetter, with his twelve-string guitar, in a 1940s publicity photograph. *(American Folklife Center)*

Huddie "Leadbelly" Ledbetter is remembered for both his twelve-string acoustic-guitar playing and his song repertoire, which draws upon nineteenth-century African American traditions. Through his connection with John A. and Alan Lomax, Leadbelly became known to the New York City political Left and emerged as one of the stars of the folk revival movement that began in the 1930s and lasted for several decades. Between 1935 and 1940, he recorded more than two hundred songs for the Lomaxes, who then placed them at the Library of Congress. This photo shows Leadbelly in his preferred attire: an immaculate pinstripe suit and bowtie.

OPPOSITE: Letter from Leadbelly to Alan and Elizabeth Lomax, November 4, 1940. *(American Folklife Center)*

The Archive of Folk Culture possesses six handwritten letters from Leadbelly to Alan Lomax, written between 1940 and 1942, which describe his life in New York City and provide insight into his relationship with the folksong collector. In this letter from November 4, 1940, Leadbelly writes of his performance at Café Society with Josh White, another fixture in the New York City folk scene.

"SWEET SINGER OF THE SWAMPLANDS"

Huddie Ledbetter
LEAD BELLY
IN
Southern Melodies

ONLY ACT PLAYING
"12 STRING GUITAR"

GUN TAP DANCING

~~36 WEST 2nd~~ STREET -:- NEW YORK CITY
604 E 9th   Nov 4 1940

Dear Mr & Mrs Lomax

How are you all to day will I hope This is the news ~~to be~~ for all we had a grand time at the cafe sicity we had so many People They didnt have seats They turn down to hundred and some People a lady by the name of Bettie Little Bought twenty five Tickets, since Then a man come for me an Josh to Play for him, for fifty Dollars a Peace a week for Three Performance a night – for Six nights a week, from Ten × two × one. fifteen minutes at a time.

ABOVE: Mexican girls sing for a Library of Congress recording, San Antonio, Texas, 1934. *(Prints and Photographs Division. Photo by Alan Lomax)*

This photograph was almost certainly taken during John A. and Alan Lomax's field trip to San Antonio, Texas, in May 1934. The girls are Josephine and Aurora Gonzalez, Pearl Manchaco, Lia Trujillo, and Adela Flores. Hastily gathered from the neighborhood by Josephine (probably at center in the photograph), they sang six songs that were issued, ten years later, on the Library's recording *Ethnic Music of French Louisiana, the Spanish Southwest, and the Bahamas*. The Lomaxes were in south Texas on a Library-sponsored trip to document Mexican American folk music.

Will Neal plays a fiddle at the Arvin Migratory Labor Camp, California, about 1940. *(The Charles L. Todd and Robert Sonkin Migrant Worker Collection. Photo by Robert Hemmig)*

In 1940 and 1941, Charles Todd and Robert Sonkin documented life in the Farm Security Administration camps of Depression-era California. Will Neal was a resident of the migratory labor camp near Arvin, California. In this photo, Sonkin (next to Neal) and Todd (with earphones) are recording Neal's fiddle music, probably in early August 1940, on a Presto disc recorder borrowed from the Library of Congress. The photographer wrote of Neal, "playing since 14 years, Will Neal . . . champion fiddler in Arvin Camp. Won many fiddlin' contests."

women. Sea shanties and railroad songs can function to lighten the burden of routine tasks and provide a rhythm that helps workers perform as a team. Lullabies bind together mother and child, and song and music of all sorts performed within the context of family help to bind one generation to the next.

Since 1976, when the American Folklife Center was created, the Folk Archive's collections have grown tremendously, both in numbers of items and breadth of coverage, to include a wide range of folklife expressions. But the signature activity at the center's Folklife Reading Room, where researchers come to use the materials, involves listening to the unparalleled collections of folk music and song, made largely in the field, from the United States and around the world. Researchers come to hear and study traditional performances of Anglo-American ballads or African American blues, work songs, and church music. They listen to railroad songs, cowboy songs, coal miners' songs, and sea chanties, or Native American music from tribes throughout North America. They study traditional music from Africa, Central and South America, the Middle East, Europe, South Asia, the Pacific, and other parts of the world.

FAR LEFT: John Galusha, known as Yankee John, at eighty-one years of age, Minerva, New York, 1940. *(Frank Warner Collection. Photo by Frank Warner)*

The folksong collectors Frank and Anne Warner first met John Galusha in August 1939, and over the next ten years recorded dozens of Irish- and Anglo-American songs from his rich repertoire. John Galusha lived with his wife Lizzie in the Adirondack town of Minerva, New York, and worked as a logger, farmer, professional guide, and forest ranger.

NEAR LEFT: Poster for a performance by Jim Garland, at the 13th Avenue Gallery, 1963. *(American Folklife Center Poster Collection)*

Jim Garland, a brother of Sara Ogan Gunning and Aunt Molly Jackson, was originally from Bell County, Kentucky. Garland's songs often chronicled attempts to unionize Kentucky miners and include "The Ballad of Harry Simms" and "I Don't Want Your Millions, Mister." He moved to New York City in the late 1930s, where he made recordings for Alan Lomax and others for the Archive of Folk-Song. Garland eventually moved to the West Coast, where he performed in 1963 at the 13th Avenue Gallery, which was probably in Portland, Oregon.

Musicians of the Haha Tribe, of Tamanar, play the *bendir* (a tambourine-shaped drum) and the *aouada* (a long-reed flute), while Paul Bowles records them, Essaouira, Morocco, August 8, 1959. *(Paul Bowles Moroccan Music Collection. Photographer unknown)*

"The most important single element in Morocco's folk culture is its music," wrote expatriate American author and composer Paul Bowles. In a land with little written literature, where illiteracy has been widespread, instrumentalists and singers have created an oral tradition. In 1959, Paul Bowles conducted extensive fieldwork documenting the folk and art music of Morocco, which was his adopted home. A man of diverse talents and unconventional ideas, Bowles is best known for his stories and novels, in particular *The Sheltering Sky* (1949). With a grant from the Rockefeller Foundation, support from the Library of Congress, and assistance from the Moroccan government, Bowles collected examples of every major Moroccan musical genre, over a period of six months, and donated his recordings to the Library of Congress.

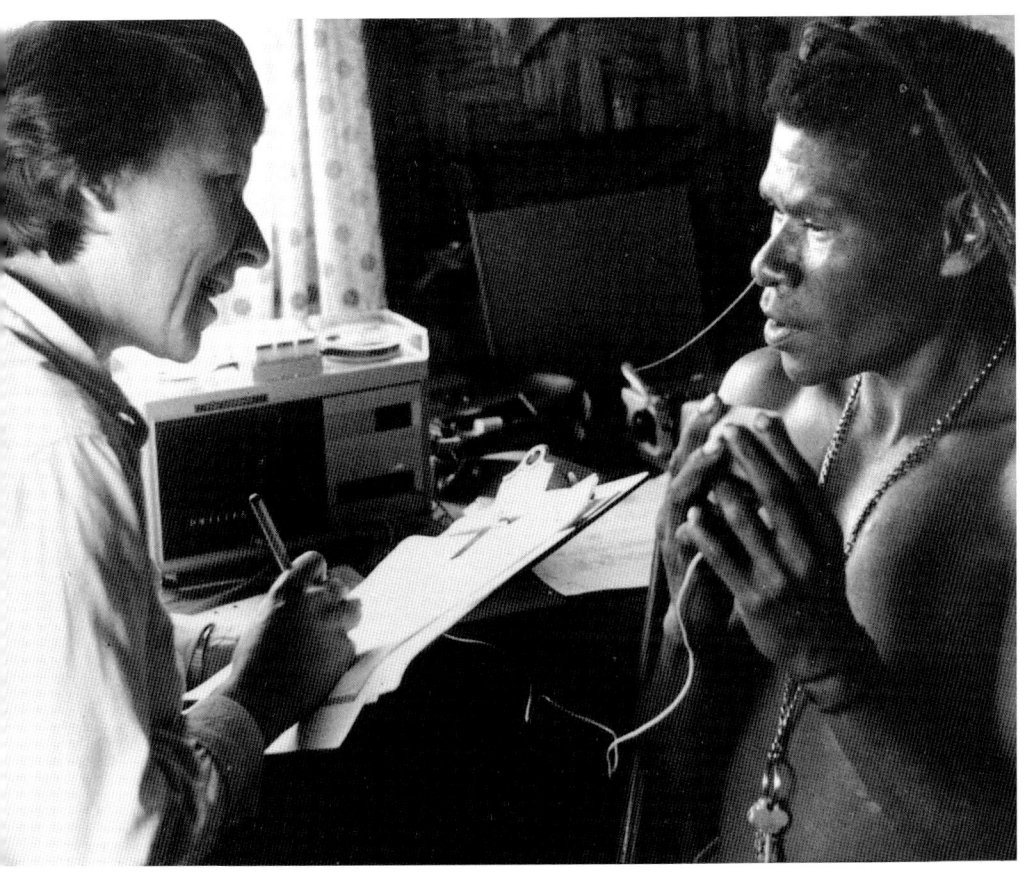

ABOVE: Ethnomusicologist Vida Chenoweth interviews Taaqiyáa, her chief Kaagú Usarufa music and text contributor, Papua New Guinea, 1967. *(Vida Chenoweth Collection. Photographer unknown)*

Donations from ethnographers whose international collecting efforts, often over a lifetime, have resulted in large collections of cultural expression from many regions and cultures, have enriched the Archive of Folk Culture. The Vida Chenoweth Collection includes audio and visual recordings, manuscripts, and photographs representing musical traditions from a variety of cultures around the world, including the music of the Usarufa people of the Eastern Highlands Province of Papua New Guinea. Featured in the collection are songs of daily life and rites of passage, dream songs, kinship songs, male cult songs, and documentation of two events known as "sing-sings."

BELOW: Portuguese *fado* musicians perform at the IV Seasons Restaurant, Lowell, Massachusetts, 1987. *(Lowell Folklife Project Collection. Photo by John Lueders-Booth)*

Fado is traditional music from Portugal, of African origin. It traveled to Lisbon from Brazil in the nineteenth century. Sung by both men and women, with a solo vocalist central to the performance, *fado* songs cover such topics as betrayal in affairs of the heart, destiny, despair, and death. The singer is usually accompanied by one Portuguese guitar and a classical guitar. In 1987, the American Folklife Center documented a range of community events and cultural expressions in Lowell, Massachusetts, primarily among the Irish, Franco-Americans, Greeks, Portuguese, Puerto Ricans, and Cambodians who make up the city's largest ethnic groups.

Story and Other Narrative Forms

Although the American Folklife Center's collections of folksong and other musical forms have received the most attention from scholars, the media, and the general public, the Folk Archive contains extensive collections of narrative materials as well, both in the form of sound recordings and as manuscripts.

Story is a principal conduit for folklore, as it is for culture in general. Stories range from ancient myths and legends, to personal-experience narratives, to the latest urban legends and e-mail hoaxes. The parables of the New Testament convey the moral and religious teachings of Jesus. Aesop's fables are didactic animal tales offering a clever illustration of a political or ethical point. Medieval romances, such as those of King Arthur, Parsifal, or Tristan and Isolde, provide narrative instruction on morals and manners. Jacob and Wilhelm Grimm collected German folktales that project the deepest values of the German people. And in Finland, Elias Lönnrot collected the stories that make up the *Kalevala* (1835), the Finnish national epic.

Likewise, in the making of the American nation, stories helped create both national and regional identities. Hero tales, such as those told of George Washington chopping down the cherry tree, Davy Crockett killing the bear, and John Henry battling the steam drill, encapsulate national mores and values. America has its "Jack Tales" from Appalachia, tales of Brer Rabbit from the American South, and coyote tales of Native American tribes. All three of these concern the trickster, a folk character who appears in different forms in different cultures, using clever tricks to outsmart his rivals or "beat the system." America has its ghost stories and other tales of the supernatural, creation stories, and animal fables.

In addition to examples of story genres mentioned here, there are in the Archive of Folk Culture many other forms of verbal lore. Poems, jokes, and riddles tell of our delight in language, and sometimes of our feelings toward outsiders. Folk drama enacts a community's values and often parodies its foibles. Children's games often include rhymes and chants. Jokes, including ethnic and racial jokes, are also part of folklore, and may be found in the Folk Archive as well.

One special field project was launched during the 1930s, largely under the aegis of the WPA Federal Writers' Project. Interviews were conducted and transcriptions made of former slaves telling their stories of life under slavery. These well-known written materials are located in the Library's Manuscript Division. About the same time, a number of folklorists, including Alan Lomax, Zora Neale Hurston, and John Henry Faulk, made sound recordings of former slaves, and over six hours of these moving narrative accounts are located in the Folk Archive, capturing the voices of those who lived through one of the darkest periods of American history.

OPPOSITE: Ben Horry, formerly a slave in South Carolina. *(Manuscript Division. Photographer unknown)*

In the 1930s, researchers working in the South for the Federal Writers' Project sought out and interviewed former slaves and recorded their words in writing. The interviewers spoke with hundreds of elderly people about their experiences of slavery. Today, these written accounts of day-to-day life give voice to the individual men and women who suffered and endured during a dark and troubling period of American history. At the same time, folklorists such as Zora Neale Hurston, Mary Elizabeth Barnicle, Alan Lomax, John and Ruby Lomax, Robert Sonkin, and John Henry Faulk were making audio recordings of former slaves, as part of both their own and WPA-sponsored collecting expeditions.

LEFT: Woody Guthrie with a guitar labeled "This Machine Kills Fascists," 1943. (New York World-Telegram and Sun Newspaper Photograph Collection, Prints and Photographs Division. Photo by Al Aumuller)

In 1940 Woody Guthrie and the Almanac Singers recorded *Songs for John Doe*, an album with clear antiwar overtones, but over the next year the sentiments of the Almanacs and many other Americans changed drastically. In 1943 Guthrie joined the Merchant Marine, and his music also took a patriotic turn, with songs like "Talking Hitler's Head Off Blues." This photograph was probably taken in 1943 as a publicity photo for *Bound for Glory*, Guthrie's autobiographical novel. Slogans similar to the one shown here appear on his instruments throughout the early 1940s—Guthrie's way of contributing to the war effort.

RIGHT: Woody Guthrie letter "Vote for Bloat," September 20, 1940. (Woody Guthrie Manuscript Collection, American Folklife Center)

By 1940 Woody Guthrie was living in New York City and enjoying one of the most productive and lucrative periods of his career. He had steady radio work, had just written "This Land Is Your Land," and had begun writing *Bound for Glory*. In March 1940, through his friendship with Alan Lomax, Guthrie came to the Archive of American Folk-Song for a three-day recording session. The memorandum asking the Librarian of Congress to pay for the session reads, "Alan Lomax has in Washington with him today and tomorrow a folk singer for whose excellence he vouches." These recordings and other products of Woody's feverish creativity are today housed at the Folk Archive. "Vote for Bloat," so titled from an illustration in the letter, is typical of Guthrie's prose style, in this case a rambling discourse about elections.

Cover and inside page of an autograph album owned by George Steinmetz, 1883. (Donated by Orville B. Craig, April 18, 1955. Duncan Emrich Autograph Album Collection)

The Duncan Emrich Autograph Album Collection comprises twenty autograph albums and ephemera dating from the turn of the twentieth century, compiled by Duncan Emrich, while he was head of the Archive of Folk-Song, from 1945 to 1955. The albums were sent to the Folk Archive in response to Emrich's request for such material on the *NBC Weekend* radio program. Albums from several families in Iowa represent a German and Anglo-American tradition that dates back to the fifteenth century. The entry shown here, addressed to George Steinmetz, contains the advice:

> Be firm when thy conscience is assailed,
> Firm when the star of hope is veiled,
> Firm in defying wrong and sin,
> Firm in life's conflicts, toil and din,
> Firm in the path by martyrs trod,
> And O, in love to man and God
> Be firm!

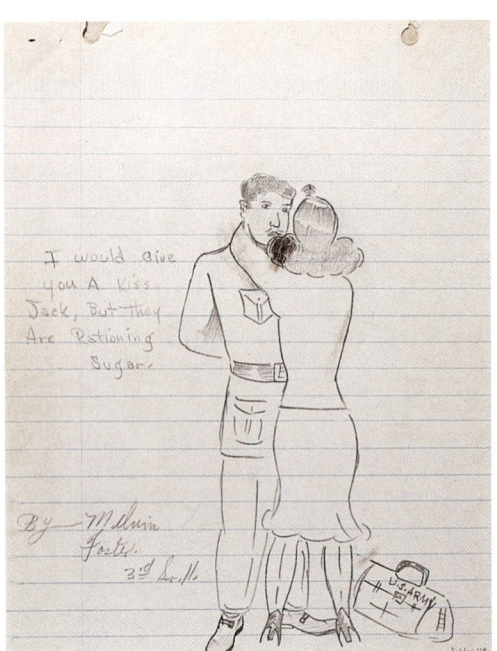

"I would give you a kiss Jack, but they are rationing sugar" by Melinda Foster, n.d., and "Food?" by Juanita Parker, 1943. (*World War II Rumor Project Collection*)

The Office of War Information (OWI) was created in 1942 to provide an "informed and intelligent understanding of the status and progress of the war effort, war policies, activities, and aims of the United States government." One project of the office was to collect rumors about the war. The papers of this project now reside at the American Folklife Center as the World War II Rumor Project Collection. High school students provided a ready source of rumors, jokes, and anecdotes about the war.

> Juanita Parker
> Eng. 6 - 3-15-43
> 3rd
> HYMAN
>
> Food?
>
> Where will the people of the United States get food? Will everybody in America starve before this war is over? These are a few of the crazy questions that the population of America are asking nowadays. Some people aren't worrying at all, because down in the cellar or way back in the closet sits dozens of cans of food stuffs.
>
> Meat is another problem so I've heard. How will meat be distributed to every family in the United States, and what kind of meat will it be? Horse? It came to my ears not so long ago, that some of our better restaurants down town have horse steak on the menu. People say that this meat is pretty good, but tough.

 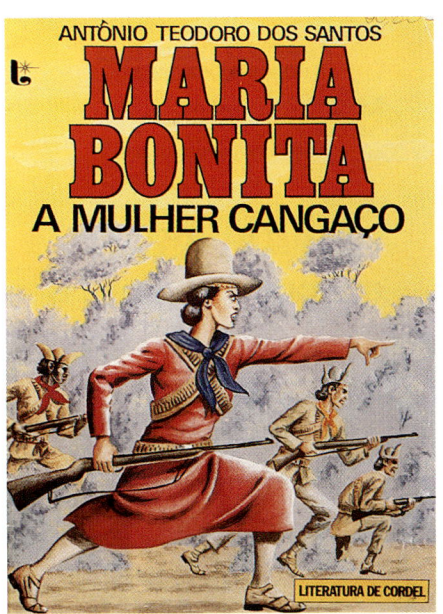

FAR LEFT: Marechal Sabóia, *Lampiões*. Lampião is a historical/mythical figure in northeast Brazil whose exploits are reminiscent of Robin Hood. *(Brazilian Chapbook Collection)*

NEAR LEFT: António Teodoro Dos Santos, *Maria Bonita: A Mulher Cangaço*. *(Brazilian Chapbook Collection)*

Not to be overlooked in the Folk Archive collections are written forms of narrative. There are many thousands of pages of manuscript materials, from researchers' field notes created during virtually every center-sponsored field project to letters written by collectors, performers, and others. One collection includes written stories, jokes, anecdotes, and rumors compiled during World War II to survey people's thoughts and feelings about the war. The government-sponsored program was designed for internal-security reasons, to find out what rumors were being spread. There is also a small but interesting collection of autograph albums from the nineteenth century and a very large collection of Brazilian chapbooks (grassroots "newspapers" containing songs, poems, and stories on a variety of topics) that continues to grow through the good auspices of the Library's Hispanic Division and the Rio de Janeiro field office.

Between 1977 and 1997, the American Folklife Center conducted fifteen field projects and cultural surveys. As a result, the archive collections are rich in narrative accounts (and other documentation) of everyday life along the Blue Ridge Parkway in Virginia and North Carolina and cowboy life and occupational culture in Montana and Paradise Valley, Nevada. Traditional agricultural practices in the Pinelands National Reserve in New Jersey are documented in narrative, as is

Brazilian chapbooks trace their origin to the poetry of medieval Europe that was transmitted orally by troubadours and minstrels. As written communication spread, this oral poetry was set to music and reproduced in handwritten chapbooks, often featuring a cover illustrated with wood-block prints. Brought to Brazil by the Portuguese in the sixteenth century, chapbooks took on the function of grassroots newspapers. Because the chapbooks were displayed outdoors, at weekly fairs, hanging from a string (*cordel*), they are called *"literatura de cordel."* The American Folklife Center's chapbook collection, the largest in the world, includes more than five thousand items, the earliest dating from the 1930s.

Fourth-graders in Blue Ridge Elementary School, Ararat, Virginia, perform a hand-clapping routine called "My Left, My Left," September 12, 1978. *(Blue Ridge Parkway Folklife Project Collection. Photo by Patrick Mullen)*

The Central Blue Ridge is a varied and dynamic region, deeply traditional and simultaneously modern. In 1978, the National Park Service engaged the help of the American Folklife Center in its plans for the cultural interpretation of the Blue Ridge Parkway. A team of field-workers talked with hundreds of people who live along the parkway and made tape recordings of conversations, storytelling, family histories, descriptions of cooking, canning, and quilting, musical performances, and church services. The team took photographs of houses, people, crops, home interiors, baptisms, and dances. This particular photograph of schoolchildren depicts one ancient and persistent form of folklore, children's games, which are often passed on orally or by imitation, in schoolyard transactions.

Acadian culture in northern Maine. Ethnic and occupational traditions in Chicago, Illinois, Paterson, New Jersey, and Lowell, Massachusetts, are described, and so is life in the Appalachian forests of West Virginia. Housewives in the Pine Barrens share their recipes for cranberries and others in western Virginia tell how to piece a quilt; a rancher in Nevada tells how cowboy life has changed over the years; a woman in Paterson tells how she came to join a union as a young girl working in the mills.

The addition of two very large collections to the Archive of Folk Culture—the International Storytelling Foundation Collection and the Veterans History Project Collection—substantially increased the representation of narrative and oral history.

The International Storytelling Foundation, located in Jonesborough, Tennessee, donated one of the largest and most important archival collections of modern storytelling in the world. The collection includes eight thousand hours of audio and video recordings, as well as photographs, manuscripts, and publications,

TOP: Jackie Torrence, a former reference librarian from High Point, North Carolina, now a professional storyteller, at the 1986 National Storytelling Festival, Jonesborough, Tennessee. *(International Storytelling Collection. Photo by Tom Raymond)*

BOTTOM: A western North Carolina farmer and traditional storyteller, Ray Hicks tells a tale at the 1983 National Storytelling Festival. *(International Storytelling Collection. Photo by Tom Raymond)*

The National Storytelling Festival, co-sponsored by the International Storytelling Center and the National Storytelling Network, has taken place each October in Jonesborough, Tennessee, since 1973, stimulating a revival in the art of storytelling. Traditionalists such as Ray Hicks tell tales alongside performers with inclinations toward social activism or experimental theater. The revival has supported, in many ways, a fledgling group of professional storytellers, among them the former reference librarian Jackie Torrence. In 2001, the American Folklife Center acquired the International Storytelling Collection, with over a quarter million items of value to both storytellers and scholars of the art.

LEFT: Color slide submitted by Nicholas W. Phillips, who served as a marine in Korea, 1952–53. *(Veterans History Project Collection. Photographer unknown)*

RIGHT: A Veterans History Project assistant, Amanda Brown sorts and arranges materials sent to the Library of Congress that document the experiences of America's war veterans. *(Photo by James Hardin)*

On October 27, 2000, the U.S. Congress mandated a new national collection of oral-history accounts of the experiences of America's war veterans and civilians who supported them. Congress unanimously passed legislation that directed the American Folklife Center to collect and preserve at the Library of Congress interviews on audio and video tape, as well as other documents, such as letters, photographs, diaries, and maps (Public Law 106–380). A searchable collections database enables comprehensive tracking of all the documentary materials received, as well as subject searching, and a National Registry of Service recognizes and honors participants by listing the names of those who contributed oral histories or other documentary materials to the developing collection.

that document every National Storytelling Festival since its founding in 1973. Performers represented in this collection include traditional storytellers, with stories that have been passed along in their families for many generations, and "professional" storytellers, with newly minted tales of their own families, experiences, and observations. Unlike the audiences of bygone days, gathered around a hearth to pass the time on a long winter night, audiences at Jonesborough and other such venues have found themselves under a tent on a bright autumn day. But the artful storyteller still has the power to entertain, delight, and, occasionally, instruct.

In October 2000, Congress unanimously passed the Veterans Oral History Act (Public Law 106–380) in order to create a collection of documentary materials at the Library of Congress honoring the nation's war veterans and those who served in support of them. "It is in the nation's best interest to collect and catalog oral histories of America's war veterans so that future generations will have original sources of information . . . and may learn of the heroics, tediousness, horrors, and triumphs of war," states the legislation. This enormous and important task was given to the American Folklife Center, which has come to be known for its expertise in collecting and preserving the cultural heritage of the American people.

"They Were Heroes But Now They're Angels." Posters attached to the wall surrounding Arlington Cemetery, across the street from the west side of the Pentagon, September 19, 2001. *(September 11, 2001, Documentary Project Collection. Photo by James Hardin)*

On September 12, 2001, the American Folklife Center sent an urgent message to folklorists and other colleagues around the country asking them to make audio recordings that documented the reactions of ordinary Americans to the tragic events of September 11, when hijacked planes crashed into the twin towers of the World Trade Center in New York City; the Pentagon, in Arlington, Virginia; and a field in rural Pennsylvania. Folklorists, anthropologists, ethnomusicologists, oral historians, and students went out into their local communities and recorded the reactions of their friends, neighbors, teachers, community leaders, police officers, and others. The idea for the project was suggested by the documentary project undertaken when Alan Lomax called on folklorists to make audio recordings of ordinary citizens commenting on their reactions to the bombing of Pearl Harbor, December 7, 1941, and the subsequent declaration of war by President Franklin Roosevelt. The September 11, 2001, Documentary Project Collection includes about six hundred taped interviews and more than two hundred photographs of spontaneous memorials from twenty-two states.

Dance

Although virtually all cultures have dance as part of their heritage, the concept of folk dance, as it has been commonly understood in the United States until recently, developed in Europe during the seventeenth century. Folk dance in Europe was customarily associated with so-called "peasant" or "folk" communities, created and choreographed collectively and anonymously, and passed on informally from generation to generation. Some English and European folk dances, as well as certain children's games, are thought to have had their origin in ancient rites, religious ceremonies, and life-cycle rituals. Maypole dances, for example, celebrate the return of spring and incorporate symbols of fertility.

The belief that folk dance is an authentic representation of an ancient heritage and the cultural identity of a folk or a nation has inspired scholars, politicians, and others to seek out typical and representative dances. For much of the twentieth century, in Western Europe and the United States, folk dancing was popular as a way to promote regional and national identity. After World War II, in the new socialist states of Eastern Europe, professional groups formed under state sponsorship to develop stylized productions of folk dance for stage presentation.

There have been attempts in the United States to identify a particular dance form as the true American folk dance. Folklorists, however, stress the inappropriateness of singling out one form of cultural expression as quintessentially American or preeminent. In our multicultural society, folk dance embraces, among others, the Anglo-American square dance, Native American fancy dance, Spanish fandango, Latin salsa, Irish jig, Bohemian polka, Scottish highland fling, African American hip-hop, and English Morris dance.

The American Folklife Center's Neptune Plaza Concert series began in 1977 and was reconstituted as "Homegrown: The Music of America" in 2002. It has featured a diverse range of music and dance traditions from this country and around the world, and many of these are documented in video, photographs, and audio recordings in the center's collections. The Blue Ridge Parkway Folklife Project, the Chicago Ethnic Arts Project, and the Maine Acadian Folklife Project documented dance traditions ranging from square dancing to polka parties.

Folklife Center collections also contain materials on the music and dance from cultural groups around the world. Notable collections include Alaskan Tlingits, Jamaican Maroons, and Moroccan Berbers. Of particular note is the Discoteca Publica Municipal de São Paulo Collection, a group of sound recordings, film footage, and photographs made in 1938 that represents one of the first ethnographic compilations of music, dance, and ritual from Brazil.

OPPOSITE: Legong dancers perform to a gamelan ensemble, Bali, 1941. *(Fahnestock South Sea Collection. Photo by Howard M. Kincheloe)*

In 1940 and 1941, Sheridan and Bruce Fahnestock, along with their wives and members of their sailing crew, conducted two expeditions to the South Seas to collect information on Pacific birds and gather specimens for exhibits at the Museum of Natural History but also to record the music of Oceania for the Fahnestock-Hubbard Foundation in New York. The Fahnestock Collection also includes film footage and still photography, such as this photograph depicting Balinese dance.

A young May queen and her courtiers around a maypole on May Day in the Cotswold village of Upper Slaughter in Gloucestershire, England, May 1, 1933. *(James Madison Carpenter Collection. Photo by Butt [Studio], Bourton)*

Originally a pre-Christian rite, the custom of erecting a maypole (with its dancing and other associated customs) flourished in England in the Middle Ages, was banned in 1644, was reinstated in 1660, and finally was revived as a children's festivity in the mid-nineteenth century. Many such customs are documented in the James Madison Carpenter Collection, considered one of the world's most important collections of British folk dance, song, and ritual drama. Carpenter was a Harvard-trained American scholar who sought out folk traditions in Britain, collecting the bulk of his material in England and Scotland from 1928 to 1935. Traversing the countryside in an Austin Seven roadster with his battery-powered Dictaphone cylinder-recording machine, a typewriter, and a camera, he documented two thousand songs, ballads, sea shanties, and carols, as well as children's singing games and three hundred mummers' plays.

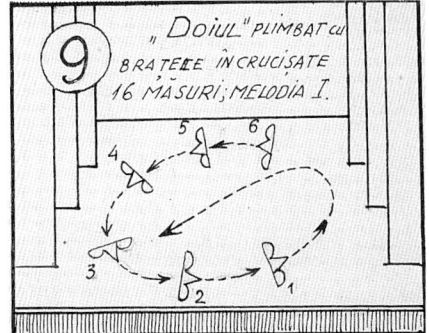

LEFT: Bridesmaids at the Sakadolskis-Pakštas wedding reception, Chicago, Illinois, June 25, 1977. *(Chicago Ethnic Arts Project Collection. Photo by Jonas Dovydenas)*

In 1977 the American Folklife Center and the Illinois Arts Council conducted a survey of more than twenty ethnic groups in Chicago to document ethnic artistic expression in that city. The resulting collection contains more than three hundred hours of sound recordings and thirteen thousand photographs. This was the first field project undertaken by the American Folklife Center, founded less than a year earlier. In this photograph, four bridesmaids dance at a Lithuanian-American wedding reception. The woman at the left is the maid of honor, as signified by her headdress.

TOP RIGHT: Drawing of Romanian dancers in rustic dress. *(Gheorghe and Eugenia Popescu-Judetz Collection. Drawing by Ada Ghinescu)*

The Gheorghe and Eugenia Popescu-Judetz Collection consists of primary documentation of Romanian folk dance and music. Dating from 1938, with the largest portion of the material from the period 1950 to 1972, the collection was donated to the American Folklife Center in 1990 and 1995 by Eugenia Popescu-Judetz. Although Romania's changing political climate and industrialization have threatened the survival of its traditions, folk dancing has remained a Romanian national pastime.

BOTTOM RIGHT: Detail of choreographic diagram for the staging of a suite, developed by Gheorghe Popescu-Judetz in 1965, based on traditional dances from the Maramures district of Romania. *(Gheorghe and Eugenia Popescu-Judetz Collection. Drawing by Gheorghe Popescu-Judetz)*

Let's Dance: The Magazine of Folk and Square Dancing, September 1954. *(Periodical Collection, American Folklife Center)*

Folk-revival clubs and organizations abound, and many publish magazines and newsletters that include a wealth of information on events, activities, and the history of particular forms of folklife expression. Many of these hard-to-find periodicals are available at the American Folklife Center.

Men's Fancy Dance Competition, Omaha Powwow, Macy, Nebraska, 1983. *(1983 Omaha Powwow Collection. Photograph by Carl Fleischhauer)*

The American Folklife Center holds documentation of Omaha Indian music from the 1890s and from the 1980s. The multiformat field collections contain forty-four wax-cylinder recordings collected by Francis La Flesche and Alice Cunningham Fletcher between 1895 and 1897, and more than three hundred songs and speeches from the 1983 Omaha harvest-celebration powwow. The powwow is a social gathering that helps to ensure the cultural conservation of Native American song and dance traditions. Dance competitions are held in various categories and prizes are awarded to the most accomplished dancers.

In December 1986, Margaret Fahnestock Lewis, of Great Mills, Maryland, presented the American Folklife Center with a collection that includes 143 sixteen-inch disc recordings of music and dance from Bali, Fiji, Java, the Kangean Islands, Madura, the Marquesas Islands, New Caledonia, Samoa, and Tahiti. These recordings were made by Mrs. Lewis's late husband, Sheridan Fahnestock, and his brother, Bruce, on two expeditions in 1940 and 1941. The collection includes documentation of Legong dancers performing to a gamelan ensemble in Bali. Accompanying the discs are five reels of color film and numerous letters, magazine articles, and newspapers clippings documenting the progress of the expeditions.

In 1949 Gheorghe Popescu-Judetz became director and choreographer of the Romanian government-sponsored Ciocîrlia Ensemble, and for the next twenty-two years (until his death in 1972) he worked on the compilation of a catalog and ethnographic description of all Romanian dances and variants. The research resulted in a collection of several thousand notated folk dance variants, more than 3,200 tape-recorded melodies, and approximately 4,000 notated dance melodies. The collection also includes musical arrangements, choreographic diagrams, photographs, and show programs documenting the activities of the Ciocîrlia and Perinitza Ensembles. Gheorghe's wife Eugenia Popescu-Judetz donated the collection to the American Folklife Center in 1990 and 1995.

Dance presents special problems for documentation, even when a video camera is available. Some researchers have developed systems of dance notation, and examples of these are available in the archive. In addition, the archive holds journals and other publications that are devoted to dance and the cultural activities surrounding dance organizations.

Djimo Kouyate, Senegalese drummers and dancers of the West African griot tradition, perform at the Library of Congress, June 5, 1986. *(Neptune Plaza Concert Series Collection. Photo by Reid Baker)*

African griot traditional dance, African American hand-dancing, Khmer classical ballet from Cambodia, Omaha Indian dance, flamenco, and English contradancing are some of the many dance traditions that have been featured on the Neptune Plaza in front of the Library's Thomas Jefferson Building and documented for the Folk Archive.

Material Culture

During the first half of the twentieth century, folklorists tended to confine their studies to (1) orally transmitted lore—especially songs, stories, legends, proverbs, and riddles—(2) certain customary traditions, such as rituals and festivals, and (3) traditions related to belief systems—luck, weather prediction, divination, and the like. Often neglected was the whole realm of human activity concerned with "craft," the traditional aspects of how objects are made and used.

Influenced by cultural anthropologists, cultural geographers, and European ethnologists, all of whom regularly included objects and the human activities and beliefs associated with them as elements of their studies, folklorists gradually came to accept what has come to be known as "material culture" as an equally valid area for documentation and analysis. Since the 1960s, American folklorists have been energetic in their studies of material culture.

American folklore studies of material culture typically address how objects are designed, made, and used, and what they mean (on various levels) to those who make and use them. Folklorists are also interested in the objects themselves, and in such matters as their shapes and dimensions, the materials from which they are made, their decorative elements, and the variations between different makers and groups, as well as variations over time and place.

Houses, barns, and other traditional buildings constitute a subcategory of material culture known as vernacular architecture. Other objects of interest include baskets, boats, clothing, furniture, metalwork, pottery, and quilts. In general, folklore studies of material culture have favored handmade objects such as these, and craftsmanship itself has been a special focus.

The Archive of Folk Culture has many collections that document material culture. The Blue Ridge Parkway Folklife Project Collection (1978) includes documentation of the quilting tradition carried on in rural communities along the Virginia–North Carolina border. The Paradise Valley Folklife Project Collection (1978–82) includes documentation of numerous objects integral to the rancher's life in northern Nevada, from boots to branding irons to saddles, all the way to ranch houses and barns. The Pineland's Folklife Project Collection (1983) includes documentation of the construction and use of traditional New Jersey bird-hunting skiffs. The Grouse Creek Cultural Survey (1985) teamed folklorists with anthropologists, sociologists, architects, and city planners to investigate the relationships among architectural history, folklife, and historic preservation. The Italian-Americans in the West Project Collection (1989–91) includes a wealth of information about Italian American material culture, including vernacular architecture, the traditional oven known as the *forno*, and various objects associated

OPPOSITE: Alma Hemmings *(left)* and folklorist Geraldine Johnson hold a "crazy quilt" from about 1948, at Mrs. Hemmings's house in Dobson, Surrey County, North Carolina, September 1978. *(Blue Ridge Parkway Folklife Project. Photo by Lyntha Eiler)*

The Folk Archive contains documentation of a number of traditional quilters from North Carolina, Virginia, Georgia, and other states, as well as documentation from the Lands' End All-American Quilt Contest (from 1992, 1994, and 1996).

NEAR RIGHT: Joe Reid, in the workshop behind his house, on Barnegat Bay, Waretown, New Jersey, 1983. *(Pinelands Folklife Project Collection. Photo by Joseph Czarnecki)*

Jersey garveys are blunt-end boats used by clammers and oystermen. Joe Reid is acknowledged locally as a master builder of these boats, which he makes and repairs. One of Reid's customers says, "A garvey's just about the ugliest thing in the world, but it makes a dynamite work boat. It's a flat-bottomed boat. It's actually a working platform."

FAR RIGHT: Dan Ramasco, Bruno Ramasco, and field-worker Howard W. (Rusty) Marshall *(left)* at the cemetery in Paradise Valley, Nevada, October 14, 1979. *(Paradise Valley Folklife Project. Photo by Carl Fleischhauer)*

Paradise Valley is the name of both a cattle-ranching valley and a crossroads community in northern Nevada's Humboldt County, where the American Folklife Center conducted an ethnographic field research project from 1978 to 1982. The focus of the project was cattle ranching but extensive work was also done on material culture, especially vernacular architecture, and the work of the immigrant Italian stonemasons. In this photo, Rusty Marshall talks with Dan and Bruno Ramasco at their grandfather's gravesite about their family and about stonemasonry.

with family-run wineries. And the Maine Acadian Cultural Survey Project Collection (1991–92) includes documentation of barns and houses that can be used to determine the geographical extent of the Acadian cultural region.

Allied to material culture is folk art, which can be defined as the use of physical items in the production of symbolic and aesthetic works by untrained artists. Folk art takes a variety of forms: painting, sculpture, multimedia displays, and assemblages, as well as the decorative aspects of otherwise utilitarian objects. Hex signs on Pennsylvania Dutch barns, tin man sculptures made by metalworkers, front yard installations and Christmas displays, decorated school lockers, carved gun stocks, and tattoos are but a few examples of this rich vein of traditional expression.

The term *folk art* is somewhat problematical and has been used to encompass a variety of productions. Folklorists and the owners of art galleries have debated the definition of folk art to an uneasy truce. Gallery owners and many museum curators tend to favor folk art objects that have fine art equivalents, such as painting and sculpture. They customarily showcase the individual image and object rather than the context within which it was made. Words such as *naive, self-taught,* and *individualistic* are used to describe these objects, and the exceptional

TOP: A twin barn in Frenchville, Maine, with connected simple gable roofs. Used for equipment storage at the time of this photograph (June 1991), the barn has additions on two sides and several wide doorways. *(Maine Acadian Folklife Project. Photo by David A. Whitman)*

RIGHT: Architectural drawing of the Joseph Delmue House, Lincoln County, Nevada. *(Italian-Americans in the West Project Collection. Drawing by Douglas L. Banks)*

Joseph Delmue was born in Biasca, Switzerland, an Italian-speaking town on the Italian-Swiss border. He emigrated to Lincoln County, Nevada, in the 1870s to cut timber for the mines at Pioche. Turning to ranching in nearby Dry Valley, in the 1880s, Delume built a substantial stone house in 1900 and a large hay barn in 1916, both buildings patterned after those in his native country. The American Folklife Center's 1990 field project Italian-Americans in the West documented with photographs and drawings buildings constructed by Italian immigrants. Vernacular architecture has been an important component of field surveys, in northern Maine, Georgia, Nevada, and along the Blue Ridge Parkway, for example, and the Folk Archive collections hold both drawings and photographs of ranch, farm, and residential buildings.

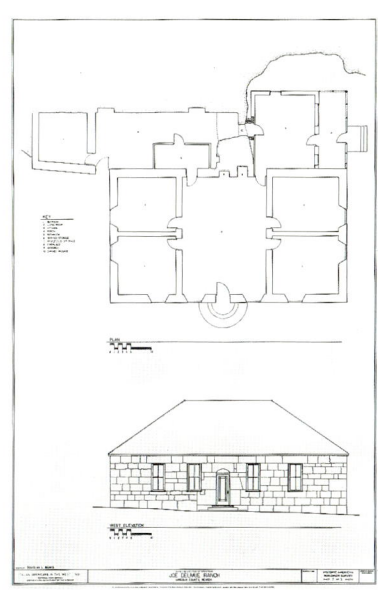

He Could Not Be Hid, painting by Howard Finster, 1978. *(American Folklife Center)*

In 1971, Howard Finster began to build and plant a garden in the two-acre yard behind his home in Summerville, Georgia, inspired by a vision instructing him to "build a paradise and decorate it with the Bible." In 1976, a similar vision prompted him to paint "sacred art," which he proceeded to do, applying to wood or metal the tractor enamel he used in his bicycle repair business. Over his lifetime, Howard Finster, "man of visions," as he called himself, worked at many occupations and trades, including farmer, textile-factory worker, sawmill laborer, and bicycle repairman. He began to preach at the age of sixteen and was eventually ordained at Violet Hill Baptist Church, in Valley Head, Alabama. He traveled from church to church, in Alabama and Georgia, until he settled at the Chelsea Baptist Church, in Menlo, Georgia. Finster is typical of many such folk or visionary artists who create fantastical sculptures and paintings, often using objects from everyday life. Finster is unusual in that he became widely known, and came to have his paintings sold at art galleries in New York and other major cities. The American Folklife Center became acquainted with the Reverend Howard Finster during a field project in south-central Georgia in 1977, and eventually commissioned Finster to paint several paintings, including *He Could Not Be Hid*.

BELOW: William Clark with the "junkyard robots" he created from recycled automotive parts, Newtonville, New Jersey, 1983. (*Pinelands Folklife Project Collection. Photo by Joseph Czarneki*)

Known as "Robot Man" in his hometown, William Clark uses the tools and skills of his trade as automotive repairman and the materials at hand in his shop to fashion robot sculptures and other artful constructions. In retirement or in their free time, workers who have developed skills in the use of materials such as wood and metal sometimes turn their hand to the creation of fanciful works of art.

ABOVE: Wall mural on 26th Street, in "Little Village," a predominately Mexican neighborhood, Chicago, Illinois, August 13, 1977. (*Chicago Ethnic Arts Project Collection. Photo by Jonas Dovydenas*) Nostalgia for their homeland may inspire immigrants to create artistic representations of distant landscapes. The outdoor mural in this photograph publicly expresses feelings shared by the community.

rather than the representative creation is featured. In fact, the folk artist is sometimes characterized as an *outsider*, *visionary*, or *idiosyncratic*, although gallery owners are loath to relinquish the magic word *folk* in advertising their work.

Just as everyone tells stories, knows the words to at least a few songs, celebrates holidays, and holds certain beliefs, all people practice some form of folk art. The everyday aspects of folk art would include the way people decorate the interiors of their homes or offices, their style of dress and body decoration, their flower gardens, and even their pencil doodlings and graffiti. The title of Kenneth Ames's book on folk art, *Beyond Necessity* (1977), goes to the heart of how folk art might be differentiated from crafts. Where crafts speak to the needs of everyday living, folk art speaks to the emotions and beliefs and the need for aesthetic satisfaction. Yet who is to say that the world of art is any less necessary to humanity than the utilitarian world?

Traditional Polish papercut artist Magdalena Gilinsky Jannotta, shown here with her work, conducted a papercut demonstration workshop at the Library of Congress in 1982. *(American Folklife Center. Photo by Carl Fleischhauer)*

The art of cutting paper may have originated in China. During the eighteenth century, German cutwork *(scherenschnitte)* and paint were combined to adorn all manner of personal messages, such as declarations of love and New Year's greetings, as well as official documents such as birth certificates and marriage licenses. Papercuts called *wycinanki* began to appear in Poland in the mid-nineteenth century, and are still used to decorate windows, joists, and other parts of the home, particularly at Christmas and Easter.

José Gonzalez (Don Ché), surrounded by his hammocks, San Sebastian, Puerto Rico, September 1, 1999. *(Local Legacies Project Collection. Photo by Giovanni Rufino)*

Through the Local Legacies project, members of Congress and private individuals across the nation were involved in celebrating the Library of Congress's Bicentennial and America's richly diverse culture. For more than a year, volunteer teams documented traditional life in their local communities, including crafts, items of produce, and events such as festivals and parades. Documentation of Puerto Rican craftsmen was submitted by Delegate Carlos Romero-Barcelo. For five hundred years, Puerto Rico has been a place of cultural fusion. This amalgamation of traditions has produced varied expressions of craftsmanship. The craft of hammock-weaving has been practiced there from the pre-Columbian era to the present. José Gonzalez, who learned from his parents, still uses the traditional maguey fiber to weave his hammocks.

Figures made in the shapes of birds, fish, rabbits, monkeys, and an assortment of flowers, made with dough and painted in bright colors, on sale at an outdoor market in the city of Quanzhou, southern Fujian province, China, 1990. *(The Nora Yeh Kemeny Family Collection. Photo by Nora Yeh)*

During the Lunar New Year or Spring Festival holiday season, folk crafts are very popular among the Chinese children of Quanzhou. American Folklife Center archivist Nora Yeh has donated her extensive collection documenting traditional Chinese arts and customs, including musical performances, both Chinese and Asian American. The collection includes sound recordings, films, photographs, color slides, manuscripts, and field notes made in Taiwan, mainland China, the Philippines, Singapore, Malaysia, Hong Kong, and the United States in the 1970s and 1980s.

Community Life and Celebration

OPPOSITE: In Wefing's Marine Supplies store, field-worker Nancy Nusz *(right)* speaks with a local engine mechanic while a store clerk looks on, Apalachicola, Florida, 1986. *(Florida Maritime Project. Photo by David A. Taylor)*

Stores such as the one shown here are often meeting places for members of the community and, in the case of this marine supply store, good sources of information about local fishing activities, practitioners, and traditions.

THE USUAL CONNOTATIONS surrounding the word *folklore*, which was coined in England by William Thoms in 1846, involve oral traditions. In the United States, when the Festival of American Folklife (now the Smithsonian Folklife Festival) was first presented on the National Mall in Washington, D.C., in 1967, and when the American Folklife Center was created by an act of Congress in 1976, the term *folklife* was recognized as one that embraced not only oral traditions but also material culture and all the community customs, traditions, and events that make up daily life. *Folklore* and *folklife* remain somewhat confusing and elusive terms. But the distinguishing characteristic of all folklife expressions is to be found in their origin within, and connection to, a particular group or community.

In general, folklife begins at home, because for most of us the immediate family constitutes our first folk group and a good deal of knowledge is conveyed within it. All the folklife expressions heretofore discussed (song and music, stories, jokes, games, dance, foodways, and material culture) can be part of family folklore, which is, of course, deeply affected by ethnicity, religion, region, and socioeconomic status. Family folklore, as a special category of experience, is often invisible to its practitioners because it consists largely of the customary practices of daily life, which are sometimes referred to by all of us offhandedly as "just the way we do things."

Family folklife includes such things as the nicknames given to children, the ways birthdays and holidays are celebrated, the planting and cultivation of a garden, practices governing the serving and eating of meals and assigning and carrying out of household chores, the arrangement of photographs in an album and the uses to which the album is put at family gatherings, and the family reunion itself, in all its agony and ecstasy. Although families may consist of mother, father, and one or more children, along with an extended family of grandparents, aunts, uncles, cousins, and miscellaneous in-laws, recent folklore studies have also examined nontraditional family groups, such as single-parent households and gay and lesbian couples. There are parallel traditions to be found in all of these family units.

The folkloric concept of "foodways" comprises the many traditional activities surrounding the production, procurement, sale, purchase, preparation, and consumption of food. Each food-related activity is itself a rich nexus for folklife study. Foodways often overlap with, for example, religious traditions—such as religious dietary restrictions, the symbolic connotations of particular items of food, or church suppers—and with occupational culture (the work of cowboys, farmers, hunters, fishermen, vintners, and shopkeepers), as well as with festivals

Engagement party for Sol Milshtein and his American fiancée, Rose, in Luboml, Poland, 1937. *(Aaron Ziegelman Foundation Collection. Photo by Lillian Ziegelman Chanales)*

Aaron Ziegelman left his hometown, Luboml, Poland, in 1938, when he was ten years old, and came to the United States with his mother and sister. One of the oldest Jewish communities in Poland, Luboml was obliterated during World War II. In 1994, Ziegelman organized a research project to engage archivists, anthropologists, and historians in the collection of information about Jewish life in Luboml, obtained from survivors and other sources. The resulting material, donated to the American Folklife Center in 2002, includes more than two thousand photographs, motion pictures, letters, maps, and oral histories that richly document everyday life in Luboml's Jewish community, capturing aspects of local schools, businesses, recreational activities, religious life, holidays, and weddings.

and other ritualized events. American Folklife Center field project collections include documentation of wine-making in California's Santa Clara Valley, ramp dinners and ginseng harvesting in West Virginia, cranberry culture in New Jersey, and oyster roasts in north Florida.

As individual family members venture out into the world, they form relationships with other people and groups who possess traditional knowledge: children in their school, sport, and social organizations; adults in their places of work, worship, and social interaction. Each purposeful and regular gathering has the possibility, to a greater or lesser degree, of developing shared traditions and, thus, becoming a folk group. Each family member may potentially become a member of, and in part derive his or her identity from, a number of different social, religious, ethnic, regional, and occupational groups and relationships.

Children may be considered as one folk group, and the complex of children's folklore and games may be approached for study in a number of ways. Play patterns are an integral part of human culture and are universal. Through play,

Pen Hing *(left)* and Sopheap Kuth celebrate their wedding at the home of Pen Hing's mother, Mrs. Chounn Chen, in Lowell, Massachusetts, September 26, 1987. *(Lowell Folklife Project Collection. Photo by John Lueders-Booth)*

The Lowell Folklife Project's examination of cultural life in an old New England mill town included study of some of the many ethnic groups represented among its citizens, especially the Irish, French, Greeks, Portuguese, Puerto Ricans, and Cambodians. Wedding ceremonies and customs, such as the Cambodian one depicted here, in which the groom follows the bride to her bedroom, bring family and friends together and educate young people about the traditions of their community.

OPPOSITE: Harvesting Spanish moss in the Atchafalaya swamp, Louisiana, 1974. *(Turner Browne Collection. Photo by Turner Browne)*

In the 1970s, Louisianan Turner Browne set himself the task of making photographs of Louisiana Cajun culture, which he feared was dying out. The resulting collection of fifteen hundred negatives and seventy-seven prints, donated to the American Folklife Center in 1999, includes such themes as Mardi Gras, foodways, horse racing, trapping, gambling, boat navigation, and socializing. The photographs offer a portrait of community life that demonstrates the intimate relationship between culture and environmental resources. The Spanish moss shown here has many uses when cured, in building construction and insulation, for example, and for stuffing mattresses and upholstered chairs.

TOP LEFT: Ray Dickens Jr. *(left)*, Kimberly Dickens, and Jeffrey Honaker on Drews Creek Road, Naoma, West Virginia, selling ramps to motorists on their way to the local annual ramp supper in 1979. *(Coal River Folklife Project. Photo by Lyntha Eiler)*

One of the first edible wild foods to appear in the Appalachian mountain region in early spring, the ramp (*Allium tricoccum*) is a type of leek that grows in the rich, dark woodlands near mountain streams. Throughout the Appalachian South, ramps are celebrated and enjoyed with suppers and festivals. The gathering and processing of ramps, as well as the suppers themselves, provide occasions for community gatherings, storytelling, and comradery. For many in the region, celebrating ramps is one of the rites of spring, and is a touchstone of a shared past and present.

TOP RIGHT: Poster for the 28th Annual Cosby Ruritan Club Ramp Festival, Cosby, Tennessee, 1981. *(American Folklife Center Poster Collection)*

The Cosby Ramp Festival claims to be the oldest of many festivals celebrating the ramp, which has been described as a cross between scallions and garlic. Founded in 1954, the festival takes place each spring on Kineauvista Hill, near Cosby, in east Tennessee. The Tennessee General Assembly acknowledged both the festival and its namesake plant in 1980 by designating a "Ramp Festival Day," resolving that "this legendary root, distinguished by odoriferous qualities, is purported to supply unyielding powers believed to have furthered the chivalrous and intrepid deeds of those who have chosen the mountains for their homes."

TOP LEFT: Weaver Maria Atiles at the Joseph Teshon Company, Inc., Paterson, New Jersey, 1994. *(Working in Paterson Project Collection. Photo by Martha Cooper)*

The occupational culture of workers in the textile and garment-manufacturing industries was documented along with many other businesses in Paterson, New Jersey, by the American Folklife Center's 1994 field project Working in Paterson, which was cosponsored by the Mid-Atlantic Regional Office of the National Park Service. Founded in 1791, Paterson was the country's first planned industrial center. At one time, it was the largest silk manufacturing center in the nation. The Working in Paterson Project Collection includes over four hundred audiotaped interviews and thousands of photographs that document how that industrial heritage expresses itself in the lives of Patersonians today.

TOP RIGHT: Harvesting cranberries at the Birches, on the Roberts Branch of the Batsto River, near Tabernacle, New Jersey, 1982. *(Pinelands Folklife Project Collection. Photo by Carl Fleischhauer)*

In 1983, the American Folklife Center conducted a field project in a region of southeastern New Jersey known as the Pine Barrens, which had been designated the Pinelands National Reserve by Congress in 1978. The Pinelands Reserve differs from national parks, forests, or monuments by virtue of safeguarding both natural and cultural resources, while maintaining patterns of compatible human use and development. People are encouraged to remain in the Pinelands Reserve and maintain their traditional patterns of land and resource use. Cranberry cultivation began in the Pine Barrens in the 1870s, and many cranberry bogs have been owned by successive generations of the same family. In the 1980s, at the time of the Folklife Center's field project, many of the workers in the cranberry bogs were from Haiti, Cambodia, and (as in this photograph) Puerto Rico.

children acquire physical and mental dexterity, as well as social skills. Games may involve ancient customs and beliefs and rituals pertaining to colors, numbers, and words. Songs and games such as "Red Rover," "Duck, Duck, Goose," and "London Bridge" have been known and played for generations, folklore passed from one child to another.

For many adults, religious belief and participation in the work of a church or religious organization are of central importance to defining identity. For some, the religious life permeates everything they do and gives meaning to a range of places and activities beyond the confines of their place of worship and the hours of devotional services. Folklorists are interested in religious customs as they are lived and experienced in everyday life, for it is religion that gives cultural significance to a multitude of objects and activities in all societies.

For many of us, the world of work occupies as much of our time as the world of family, and some of us spend more waking hours at the office, studio, or factory than we do at home. Like the home, these workplaces, with their opportunities for sustained social interaction, create traditions that are shared and passed on to new generations of workers. Initial folkloric interest in work grew out of the Industrial Revolution and the desire to study earlier ways of life and modes of economic production. In the United States, students were particularly attracted to the resource-based trades that established regional and national identities linked to raw materials, such as mining, fishing, building construction, ranching, and logging. Such a list informed the Folklife Center's Italian-Americans in the West Project, for example, with its examination of occupation in five western states. Center studies of occupation and culture have also been conducted in Paterson, New Jersey, north Florida, and southern West Virginia. Likewise, occupation was a large consideration in many of the collections made during the 1930s New Deal projects. Documentation of farmers, factory workers, fishermen, waitresses, shopkeepers, and many others formed a historical record of everyday work during the Great Depression.

One American Folklife Center project focused attention on grassroots community traditions nationwide. As part of the celebration of the Bicentennial of the Library of Congress in 2000, Librarian James H. Billington suggested a project that came to be known as Local Legacies. The Library invited U.S. senators and representatives to identify "signature" traditions and activities from their states and districts; document them in photographs, sound recordings, and written reports; and send a portion of that documentation to the American Folklife Center for inclusion in the Archive of Folk Culture. The resulting

Rancher Les Stewart, Ninety-Six Ranch, Paradise Valley, Nevada, 1980. *(Paradise Valley Folklife Project Collection. Photo by Carl Fleischhauer)*

The American Folklife Center holds extensive documentation of cowboy life in Montana, Utah, and Nevada and has published several books and produced a major exhibition, *The American Cowboy* (1983), on the subject. Les Stewart, himself a historian of ranch life in Nevada, and his family were especially welcoming to field workers during the Paradise Valley Folklife Project.

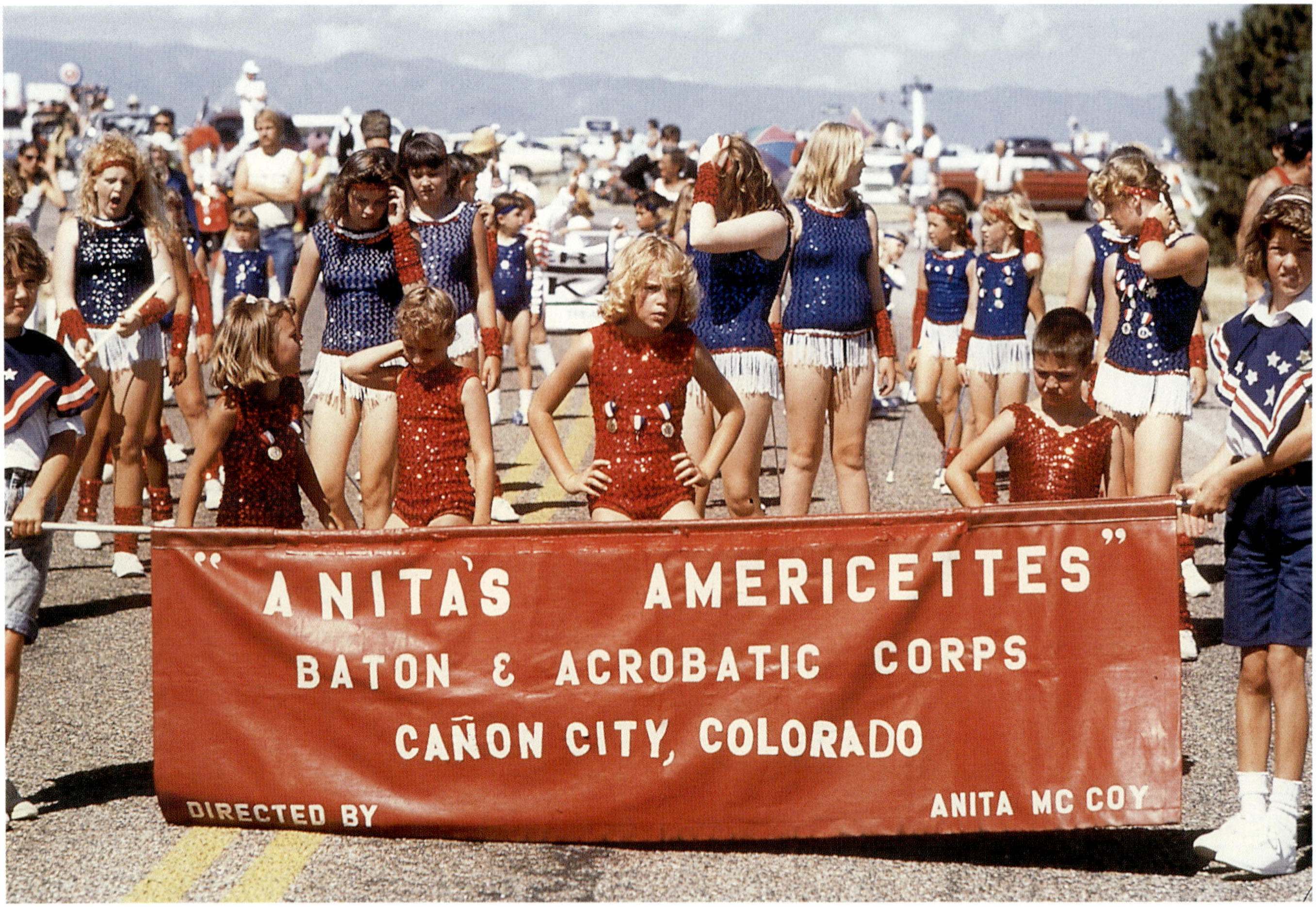
"ANITA'S AMERICETTES"
BATON & ACROBATIC CORPS
CAÑON CITY, COLORADO
DIRECTED BY
ANITA MC COY

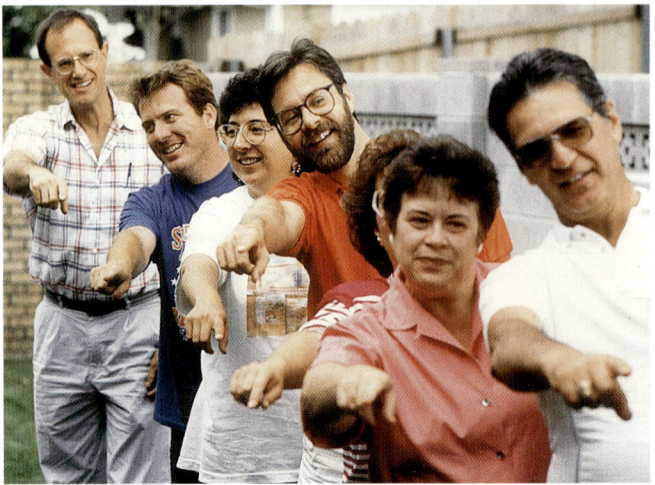

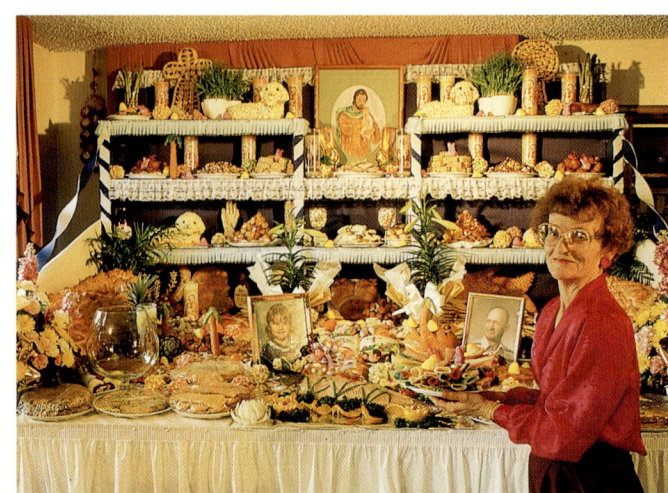

OPPOSITE TOP: Fourth of July parade, Pueblo, Colorado, 1990. *(Italian-Americans in the West Project Collection. Photo by Ken Light)*

OPPOSITE BOTTOM LEFT: Family and visitors join in playing a game of "Where's the Bear," during a Fourth of July Celebration at the home of Al and JoAnna Collette, Pueblo, Colorado, 1990. *(Italian-Americans in the West Project. Photo by Ken Light)*

OPPOSITE BOTTOM RIGHT: Josephine Martellaro of Pueblo, Colorado, with the Saint Joseph's Day table she created at her home in 1990. *(Italian-Americans in the West Project. Photo by Myron Wood)*

In July 1990, a team of folklorists for the Italian-Americans in the West Folklife Project studied the social, occupational, and religious traditions of the Italian American community in Pueblo, Colorado, and interviewed members of local families, such as Al and JoAnna Collette. The Collettes had established their business, Collette Catering and Carry Out, as a way to involve their children in their daily lives, and six of the seven worked for the catering service. Collette Catering was often called upon to prepare foods for the St. Joseph's Day table ritual, a tradition brought from Sicily in which parishioners prepare an elaborate feast in gratitude to St. Joseph for his intercession on their behalf. The Collettes invited the Folklife Center field team to spend the Fourth of July with the family, for food, fun, and fireworks. After supper, folklorists and family members joined in playing a number of games, including "Simon Says" and "Where's the Bear."

LEFT: Foxhunters in the New Jersey Pine Barrens, 1980. *(Pinelands Folklife Project Collection. Photo by Mary Hufford)*

In the United States, there are two major traditions of foxhunting: the English style, in which participants mounted on horses "ride to the hounds" in pursuit of the fox; and a less formal style, in which dog owners drive pick-ups and station themselves at listening points in order to hear the musical baying of their hounds as they chase the fox.

Crow Fair campgrounds, Crow Agency, Montana, August 1979. *(Montana Folklife Survey Collection. Photo by Michael S. Crummett)*

Held in various forms and venues throughout the country, the intertribal powwow is a contemporary social gathering centered around dancing. At encampments, such as the one shown in this aerial photograph, the powwow lasts from several days to a week, and people live in a traditional tent village. The symbolic center of the event is the drum, a name that applies both to the instrument and to the group of musicians who play it. Traditional dancing, regalia, foods, and games figure in the gathering, and children thus learn the traditional ways of their parents and ancestors.

collection, Billington suggested, would provide a snapshot of traditional cultural life in America at the end of the twentieth century.

The American Folklife Center contacted folklorists in every state to solicit their help and participation. Congressional enthusiasm and response far exceeded expectations, with about 90 percent of the Senate and over 70 percent of the House of Representatives nominating projects in their home districts. Festivals, historic sites, civic activities, occupational culture, environmental projects, and artists and craftsmen were nominated and documented. Box after box of materials arrived at the center, with documentation of community barbecues, parades, trail rides, and folk music festivals. The Local Legacies Project Collection consists of more than eight hundred projects that illustrate and showcase community culture in America.

Thus does the work of building the Folk Archive proceed, this "national project with many workers." Across the United States, a panoply of events and activities bears witness to the endless capacity of the American people to celebrate themselves in creative, ingenious, and fanciful ways. These are the folklife expressions that Americans have themselves designated and documented as their "local legacies" to the future.

BOTTOM LEFT: Program for the 22nd National Folk Festival, Oklahoma City, Oklahoma, June 1957. *(National Council for the Traditional Arts Collection)*

The National Folk Festival was first held in 1934, in St. Louis, Missouri, the brainchild of Sarah Gertrude Knott, a woman of vision and determination. Knott's intention was to bring together "groups from different sections of the country with their folk music, dances, and plays, to see what their story would tell of our people and our country." Over the years, the festival was held in many different locations, from Dallas, Texas, to Washington, D.C. Documentation of the festivals has resulted in a huge collection of material, comprising over forty-seven hundred hours of recorded performances. Under a cooperative agreement with the National Council for the Traditional Arts (the umbrella organization for the festival), the collection is being copied for preservation and access, cataloged, and transferred to the American Folklife Center.

BOTTOM RIGHT: The yellow ribbon that Penne Laingen tied around an oak tree in the front yard of her Bethesda, Maryland, home in 1979. *(American Folklife Center)*

The provenance of the recent tradition of displaying yellow ribbons to express support for absent loved ones dates to November 4, 1979, when Penne Laingen tied a ribbon around an "old oak tree" in her front yard, to symbolize her determination that her husband, Bruce, who was being held hostage in Iran at the time, would return home safely. Mrs. Laingen pledged that her yellow ribbon would remain in place until her husband, the acting ambassador to Iran, took it down himself. A combination of media attention and the creation of a support organization, the Family Liaison Action Group (FLAG), which adopted the yellow ribbon as its symbol, brought the yellow ribbon to national attention. Its display caught on for a variety of similar occasions and in a variety of forms and manifestations.

CENTER: Ceremony to commemorate the birthday of Confucius, at an elementary school in Chinatown in Los Angeles, Californian, 1984. *(Nora Yeh Kemeny Family Collection. Photograph by Nora Yeh)*

Although this ritual dance in honor of Confucius, who is known as the "Supreme Saint and Master Educator," is traditionally performed in a Confucian temple, by both boys and girls, this particular ceremony took place in a school. The performance was accompanied by Chinese instruments of eight different types. The event was supported by the government of Taiwan to promote education and help preserve this ancient Chinese cultural tradition within the Los Angeles community.

TOP: "Columbus Landing Ceremony," Columbus Day Celebration, San Francisco, California, 1989. *(Italian-Americans in the West Project Collection. Photo by Ken Light)*

Columbus Day parades began in San Francisco in 1869, and since 1885 the local Italian American community has produced elaborate Columbus Day parades and pageants to celebrate its ethnic identity. After World War I, the annual celebration came to include a variety of events, such as the mock landing of Columbus in the New World, staged from fishing boats in the harbor; the selection of a pageant queen, "Queen Isabella"; and the impersonation of Columbus by a succession of Italian American men. In 1989, the Columbus Landing Ceremony was held at Aquatic Park, in San Francisco, with the U.S. Navy Band providing music and Joseph Cervetto Jr. playing the part of Christopher Columbus, a role that his father had taken before him.

BOTTOM: Dressed in a feather cape, the "king" (or Mo'i) is surrounded by his "royal court." Halema'uma'u Crater, Aloha Festival, Volcanoes National Park, Hawaii, August 1994. *(Local Legacies Project Collection. Photo by Ric Noyle)*

An annual statewide festival, begun in 1946, celebrates the pageantry of ancient Hawaiian culture and today's multiculturalism. In 1999, more than thirty thousand volunteers helped put on three hundred events on six islands, and about one million people attended. The theme was "Hui Pu I Ka Hula" (together in song and dance), chosen to strengthen awareness of cultural heritage.

Street procession staged by Nueva Esperanza Church, Lowell, Massachusetts, April 1, 1988. *(Lowell Folklife Project Collection. Photo by John Lueders-Booth)*

In 1987, the American Folklife Center launched a year-long study of traditional arts and culture in Lowell, Massachusetts, in cooperation with the Lowell Historic Preservation Commission, looking in particular at the creation and uses of community space. Lowell is a city of more than fifty ethnic groups, and a succession of immigrants have relocated to the city. Ethnic and cultural identities are intimately connected with place, and when cultural groups relocate they find ways to make their new home their own. In this photograph, parishioners of Nueva Esperanza Church stage their annual enactment of the Passion of Christ on Good Friday. By mapping a sacred route, the via dolorosa of ancient Jerusalem, onto the secular cityscape, they transform the old mill town into a reflection of their Catholic faith.

For Further Reading

Bartis, Peter T. "A History of the Archive of Folk Song at the Library of Congress: The First Fifty Years." Ph.D. diss., University of Pennsylvania, 1982.

Bradunas, Elena, and Brett Topping, eds. *Ethnic Heritage and Language Schools in America.* Washington: Library of Congress, 1988.

Brunvand, Jan Harold. *American Folklore: An Encyclopedia.* New York and London: Garland Publishing, 1996.

Carter, Tom, and Carl Fleischhauer. *The Grouse Creek Cultural Survey: Integrating Folklife and Historic Preservation Field Research.* Washington: Library of Congress, 1988.

Eiler, Lyntha Scott, Terry Eiler, and Carl Fleischhauer. *Blue Ridge Harvest: A Region's Folklife in Photographs.* Washington: Library of Congress, 1981.

Gray, Judith. "American Folklife Center." In *Many Nations: A Library of Congress Resource Guide for the Study of Indian and Alaska Native Peoples of the United States.* Edited by Patrick Frazier. Washington: Library of Congress, 1996.

Gross-Bressler, Sandra. "Culture and Politics: A Legislative Chronicle of the American Folklife Preservation Act." Ph.D. diss., University of Pennsylvania, 1995.

Hardin, James. "American Folklife Center." In *American Women: A Library of Congress Guide for the Study of Women's History and Culture in the United States.* Edited by Sheridan Harvey, et al. Washington: Library of Congress, 2001.

Hufford, Mary. *One Space, Many Places: Folklife and Land Use in New Jersey's Pinelands National Reserve.* Washington: Library of Congress, 1986.

Jabbour, Alan. "The American Folklife Center: A Twenty-Year Retrospective." *Folklife Center News* 18: 1–2 (winter–spring 1996), part 1, pp. 3–19; 18:3–4 (summer–fall 1996), part 2, pp. 3–23.

Kodish, Debora. *Good Friends and Bad Enemies: Robert W. Gordon and the Study of American Folksong.* Urbana and Chicago: University of Illinois Press, 1986.

Marshall, Howard W., and Richard E. Ahlborn. *Buckaroos in Paradise: Cowboy Life in Northern Nevada.* Washington: Library of Congress, 1980.

Porterfield, Nolan. *Last Cavalier: The Life and Times of John A. Lomax, 1867–1948.* Urbana and Chicago: University of Illinois Press, 1996.

Taylor, David A., and John Alexander Williams. *Old Ties, New Attachments: Italian-American Folklife in the West.* Washington: Library of Congress, 1992.

OPPOSITE: Huskies on the trail, Iditarod Trail Sled Dog Race, Alaska, March 1988. *(Local Legacies Project. Photo by Jeff Schultz)*

Called "the last great race on earth," Alaska's Iditarod pits dog teams and their mushers against the rugged Alaskan wilderness. Each team must cover more than one thousand miles, from Anchorage in the south to Nome in the north. For two weeks they face subzero temperatures, long hours of darkness, blinding winds, and treacherous climbs. The challenges presented by these harsh conditions reflect Alaska's heritage of survival in the midst of wild, untamed nature.

Music and Spoken Word from the Archive of Folk Culture

AUDIO RECORDINGS ON CD

Produced by Jennifer Cutting with selection assistance from Judith Gray, Todd Harvey, Ann Hoog, Michael Taft

Staff engineer: Jonathan Gold

Mastering engineer: Charlie Pilzer (Airshow Mastering)

Disc transfers: Brittany Muehl, Larry Appelbaum, James Sam (Cutting Corporation)

Digital conversion: Peter Alyea

Additional assistance: Matthew Barton, Marcia K. Segal

Total time: 73:29

OPPOSITE: Margaret O. Moody sings for Anne Grimes, Chillicothe, Ohio, September 9, 1955. *(Anne Grimes Collection. Photo by James Grimes)*

In the 1950s, Anne Grimes documented vestiges of traditional singing and dulcimer playing in central and southeastern Ohio, where she lived, in photographs and recordings. Here, Margaret O. Moody sings a song learned from her family, who first settled in Ohio in the early 1800s.

A selection of recordings from the Archive of Folk Culture is included here as an audio companion to help bring to life the images and descriptions in the Illustrated Guide. Taken together, these voices and images provide a representative sampling of the myriad tradition-bearers documented in the Folk Archive: young and old, rural and urban, immigrant and native. Many are excerpts from longer recordings and some have been edited. They are arranged on the disc in order of their mention in the text. For each selection, AFS, AFC, and particular item numbers are provided to enable researchers to find the complete versions of the original recordings in the archive.

The recordings selected for this CD, like the majority of recordings in the Folk Archive, are field recordings, with all the attendant background noises of work, home, and street life. They are the aural equivalent of candid snapshots, as opposed to staged studio portraits. Some were made by trained recordists and others by amateurs using less-than-perfect microphone placement or recording levels. Early recordings were made using the technologies of their day, such as wax cylinder recorders or acetate disc cutters. For every selection, we have tried to enhance the listening experience by editing out the more distracting clicks, pops, and hisses. Despite the faults inherent in obsolete recording technologies and less-than-perfect field conditions, each of these recordings retains a sense of the vibrant life of its maker and its subject.

1. "Roll the Old Chariot Along" and "Haul the Woodpile Down." (0:57) *Photo of collector on page 5.* Singers unknown. Sea shanties recorded by Robert W. Gordon in the San Francisco Bay Area of California in the early 1920s. Gordon Cylinder Collection, cylinder 50, AFC 1928/002: AFS 18,995 A

2. "Manabus Tells the Ducks to Shut Their Eyes." (1:23) *Photo of collector on page 9.* Sung by Louis Pigeon. One of many legends concerning the culture hero Manabus. In this story, he tricks ducks into dancing with their eyes closed by promising to sing them his songs, then wrings their necks one by one until one bird peeks, and they escape. Recorded by Frances Densmore in Keshena, Wisconsin, July-August 1925. Frances Densmore Menominee Cylinder Collection, AFC 1952/001: AFS 10,687 B5

3. "For to Drive My Father's Cows" and "British Grenadiers." (1:18) *Photo on page 11.* Sung and played on the fiddle by Carrie B. Grover. Recorded by Eloise Hubbard Linscott in Gorham, Maine, 1943. Eloise Hubbard Linscott Collection, AFC 1942/002: AFS 28,143 A1-2

4. "Rocky My Soul." (1:38) *Photo on page 12.* Sung by Uncle Rich Brown. Recorded by John A. and Ruby T. Lomax in Sumterville, Alabama, October 1940. John and Ruby Lomax 1940 Southern States Recording Trip Collection, AFC 1940/003: AFS 4027 B1

5. "Mr. Phonograph." (1:11) *Text on page 14.* Jesse Walter Fewkes talking to the new Edison cylinder recording machine in order to demonstrate its capabilities to a visiting Passamaquoddy man. Probably recorded in Boston, late 1890–early 1891. Jesse Walter Fewkes Passamaquoddy Cylinder Collection, AFC 1972/003: AFS 14,737 B15

6. "Shove It Over." (2:35) Sung by Zora Neale Hurston, with spoken commentary. Track-lining song learned by Hurston from Charlie Jones on a railroad construction camp near Lakeland, Florida, in 1933. Recorded by Herbert Halpert for the Federal Writers Project in Jacksonville, Florida, June 18, 1939. Herbert Halpert / Southern Recording Trip 1939 Collection, AFC 1939/005: AFS 3136 A1

7. "Old Uncle Rabbit" and "Sea Lion Woman." (1:19) *Photo of collector on page 15.* Sung by Christine and Katherine Shipp. "Sea Lion Woman" was featured in the 1999 Paramount film *The General's Daughter*. Recorded by Herbert Halpert in Byhalia, Mississippi, May 13, 1939. Herbert Halpert / Southern Recording Trip 1939 Collection, AFC 1939/005: AFS 3008 A1 and B3

8. Dance song with solo vocal. (2:00) *Text on page 16.* Bambara dance music performed on *balaphons* (gourd-resonated xylophones) and hand drums by an ensemble of professional musicians, with solo vocal by local singer "Lizahbet." Recorded by Arthur S. Alberts in the "pagan" (non-Muslim) quarter of the city of Bobo-Dioulasso, Burkina Faso (formerly Upper Volta), 1949. Arthur S. Alberts Collection, AFC 1953/008: AFS 10,754 A9

9. "Jesus Leads Me All the Way." (3:43) *Photo of collector on page 17.* Sung with stamping and clapping by Reverend Goodwin and the Zion Methodist Church congregation. Because slaves were forbidden to drum, the Gullah style evolved with singers stamping and clapping rhythmic accompaniment. In this recording, singers stamp (and later clap) on the beat. Toward the end, however, they shift abruptly to a syncopated clapping pattern while their singing remains unsyncopated, a superb example of the survival of African polyrhythms in the New World. Recorded by Henrietta Yurchenco in John's Island, South Carolina, March 29, 1970. Henrietta Yurchenco / John's Island Collection, AFC 1996/066: 1

10. Helen Hartness Flanders / "The Farmer's Curst Wife." (3:52) *Photo on page 18.* Duncan Emrich introduces Vermont folksong collector Helen Hartness Flanders, who in turn introduces Asa Davis, an Irish-American singer from Vermont. Davis was one of three singers who performed at a lecture and concert entitled "New England Balladry," presented by Flanders in the Coolidge Auditorium of the Library of Congress in Washington, D.C., on February 27, 1948. Helen Hartness Flanders Collection, AFC 1948/001: AFS 9127 A

11. Reactions to the Bombing of Pearl Harbor. (1:39) *Text on page 18.* Recorded by Philip Cohen and Alan Lomax in Washington, D.C., December 8, 1941. "Man-on-the-Street" Interviews Collection, AFC 1941/004: AFS 6358 A

12. "White as Snow." (1:45) *Text on page 20.* Riddles spoken by Maggie Hammons Parker, with comments by Alan Jabbour. Recorded by Alan Jabbour and Carl Fleischhauer in Marlinton, West Virginia, April 23, 1972. Hammons Family Collection, AFC 1972/014: AFS 14,722 A3

13. "White House Blues." (2:50) *Photo on page 24.* Alan Jabbour introduces the American Folklife Center's first Neptune Plaza Concert: a performance by the Bluegrass Cardinals, featuring Don Parmley (banjo), David Parmley (guitar), Randy Graham (lead vocal, mandolin), Warren Blair (fiddle), and John Davis (bass). Recorded by the Library of Congress on the steps of the Thomas Jefferson Building, April 25, 1977. Neptune Plaza Concert Series Collection, AFC 1977/003: AFS 18,983

14. "Tom Dooley." (0:46) *Photo on page 29.* Sung by Frank Proffitt Sr. Recorded by Frank Warner in Beech Mountain, North Carolina, 1940. Anne and Frank Warner Collection, AFC 1950/002: AFS 15,264 A2

15. "A Young Man's Love" / "With His Old Gray Beard A-Shining." (1:49) *Related text on page 32.* "Young Man's Love" sung by Gloria Trail. "Old Grey Beard" sung by

Reba and Wilma McDonald. Recorded by Vance Randolph in Farmington, Arkansas, October 1941. Vance Randolph Collection, AFC 1941/001: AFS 5286 A2 and B2

16. "Soldier's Joy." (2:08) *Photo on page 33.* Played on tenor banjo by Myrtle B. Wilkinson and on fiddle by Mrs. Ben Scott. Recorded by Sidney Robertson Cowell in Turlock, California, October 31, 1939. Sidney Robertson Cowell California Folk Music Project Collection, AFC 1940/001: AFS 4772 A2

17. "Hijo, Hijo, Mira Esta Muher." (0:34) *Photo on page 35.* Children's game song sung by Josephine and Aurora Gonzalez, Pearl Manchaco, Lia Trujillo, and Adela Flores. Recorded by John A. and Alan Lomax in San Antonio, Texas, May 1934. John A. and Alan Lomax 1934-35 Southern States Recording Trip Collection, AFC 1935/002: AFS 10 A1

18. "Figure Eight," done to the tune of "Sally Goodin." (1:40) *Photo of collectors on page 36.* Square dance with Walter King (caller), Willard Brewer (fiddle), and Red Harmon (guitar). Recorded by Charles L. Todd and Robert Sonkin at Shafter FSA migrant labor camp, Shafter, California, August 4, 1940. The Charles L. Todd and Robert Sonkin Migrant Worker Collection, AFC 1985/001: AFS 4114 A1

19. Chorus and dance. (1:07) *Photo on page 38.* Sung and played by Rais Mahamad ben Mohammed and ensemble, musicians of the Haha tribe in Tamanar. Recorded by Paul Bowles in Essaouira, Morocco, August 8, 1959. Paul Bowles Moroccan Music Collection, AFC 1960/001: AFS 11,625 3B

20. "Já Estas Com os Copos" ("You're Already Drunk, Don't Drink Any More"). (2:52) *Photo on page 39.* Musicians Olivete Maria (singer), Mário Bulhões (acoustic guitar), and Duarte Tavares (Portuguese guitar), performing a song from the Portuguese *fado* tradition at the IV Seasons Restaurant in Lowell, Massachusetts. Recorded by Barbara Fertig in Lowell, Massachusetts, November 14, 1987. Lowell Folklife Project Collection, AFC 1987/042: LFP-BF-R001

21. "Whipping a Slave." (1:10) *Text on page 41.* Interview with Laura Smalley about the days of slavery. Recorded by John Henry Faulk in Hempstead, Texas, 1941. John Henry Faulk Texas Recordings Collection, AFC 1941/016: AFS 5496 A and B

22. "The Golden Arm." (1:18) *Photo on page 47.* Excerpt from a story told by North Carolina storyteller Jackie Torrence. Recorded at the 1986 National Storytelling Festival, Jonesborough, Tennessee. International Storytelling Collection, AFC 2001/008: 83FEJC01 A1

23. "The Heifer Hide." (2:21) *Photo on page 47.* Excerpt from a "Jack tale" told by North Carolina farmer and storyteller Ray Hicks. Recorded at the 1990 National Storytelling Festival, Jonesborough, Tennessee. International Storytelling Collection, AFC 2001/008: 90FEPT11

24. "Mad, Glad, Sad." (2:46) *Text on page 48.* Interview with veteran James F. Walsh, who was a gunner in the Korean War. Recorded by J.G. Webb in Chicago, Illinois, on September 9, 2003. Veterans History Project Collection, AFC 2001/001/1939

25. Reactions to the terrorist attacks on September 11, 2001. (4:08) *Text on page 49.* Interview with Lillie Haws, owner of a New York City bar, conducted by Sarah Phillips in New York City, on November 12, 2001. September 11, 2001, Documentary Project Collection, AFC 2001/015: SR297

26. "Tabuh Gari." (2:03) *Photo on page 50.* Played by the *gamelan semar pegulingan* ensemble, or "love gamelan" named for Semar, the god of love. Recorded by the Fahnestock South Sea Expedition in Ubud [Teges], Bali, in 1941. Fahnestock South Sea Collection, AFC 1986/033: AFS 25,863 A

27. "Constant Billy." (1:02) *Related text on pages 51–52.* Sung and fiddled by Morris dance musician Sam Bennett, from the village of Bampton-in-the-Bush, Oxfordshire. Recorded by James Madison Carpenter on Dictaphone cylinder in Bampton, England, in 1933. James Madison Carpenter Collection, AFC 1972/001: AFS 19,903.

28. "Grand Entry Song." (3:08) *Related text on page 54.* "Grand Entry" is the name for the occasions in which all of the powwow dancers enter the arena, announced by an emcee as they arrive. Rufus White translates

the song: "Our relatives are making their way into the arena. God, please watch over us." Words include, "Pity us, and look at us, and watch over us." Played by the Host Drum. Recorded by Carl Fleischhauer at the 1983 Omaha powwow in Macy, Nebraska. 1983 Omaha Powwow Collection, AFC 1986/038: 0388

29. "They Was Made Out of Scraps." (2:08) *Photo on page 56.* Interview with quilter Alma Hemmings recorded by Geraldine Johnson in Dobson, North Carolina, on September 19, 1978. Blue Ridge Parkway Folklife Project Collection, AFC 1982/009: AFS 21,504: BR8-GJ-R68

30. "My Father Can Remember." (1:33) *Photo on page 70.* Interview on the history of Pinelands cranberry harvesting with Mark Darlington, whose father invented a type of dry harvester and later developed the wet harvester. Recorded by Mary Hufford in Whitesbog, New Jersey, in November 1983. Pinelands Folklife Project Collection, AFC 1991/023: AFS 23,869: PFP83-AMH015

31. "I Made All My Children's Dresses." (1:08) *Related text on page 70.* Interview with retired garment worker Rose Vecchierella about the sewing she did at home for her family. Recorded by David Taylor in West Paterson, New Jersey, on August 9, 1994. Working in Paterson Project Collection, AFC 1995/028: WIP-DT-A009

32. "Why Rancher Les Stewart Shuns New Technology for Branding." (0:56) *Photo on page 71.* Interview with Les Stewart videotaped by Carl Fleischhauer and William A. Wilson at the Ninety-Six Ranch, Paradise Valley, Nevada, on May 9, 1981. Paradise Valley Folklife Project, AFC 1991/021: NV81-VT4

33. "The Donkey's What Carried Mary to the Inn." (3:42) *Text on page 73.* Interview with Al and JoAnna Collette on the St. Joseph's Day foods in their family recipe book. Recorded by Paula Manini and Paola Tavarelli in Pueblo, Colorado, on June 24, 1990. Italian Americans in the West Collection, AFC 1989/022: IAW-PM-A002

34. "Welcoming the Spirit of the Sage." (2:40) *Photo on page 76.* The Confucian Ritual Orchestra from Taiwan performs a ceremony to commemorate the birthday of Confucius at Castelar Elementary School in Chinatown in Los Angeles, California. Recorded by Nora Yeh on October 27, 1984. Nora Yeh Kemeny Family Collection, AFC 2000/018

35. "Unconstant Lover." (1:36) *Photo on page 81.* Sung by Margaret O. Moody. Recorded by Anne Grimes in Chillicothe, Ohio, on September 9, 1955. Anne Grimes Collection, AFC 1996/003 21A

Bonus Track:

"The United States Needs Prayer, Everywhere." (2:21) Sung by Lulu Morris and the congregation of the African Methodist Church. Recorded by Herbert Halpert in Tupelo, Mississippi, in May 1939. Herbert Halpert / Southern Recording Trip 1939 Collection, AFC 1939/005: AFS 2959 B1